OTHER BOOKS BY THE AUTHOR

*The Amazing Power of Grace

*Authority of the Excellent name of Jesus

The Amazing of Power of Faith

FAITH
YOUR
SEVENTH-SENSE

HUMPHREY O. AKPARAH

authorHOUSE®

AuthorHouse™ LLC
1663 Liberty Drive
Bloomington, IN 47403
www.authorhouse.com
Phone: 1-800-839-8640

Published by AuthorHouse 07/30/2014

ISBN: 978-1-4969-0208-5 (sc)
ISBN: 978-1-4969-0207-8 (e)

SIXTEEN (16) DIFFERENT BIBLE TRANSLATIONS USED IN THE BOOK:
FAITH YOUR SEVENTH-SENSE
1.   KING JAMES VERSION
2.   NEW KING JAMES VERSION
3.   NEW INTERNATIONAL VERSION
4.   J.B. PHILLIPS [NEW TESTAMENT]
5.   NIV READERS VERSION
6.   COMMON ENGLISH BIBLE
7.   CONTEMPORARY ENGLISH VERSION
8.   GOD'S WORD TRANSLATION
9.   GOOD NEWS TRANSLATION
10. HOLMAN CHRISTIAN STANDARD BIBLE
11. EXPANEDED BIBLE
12. NEW LIFE VERSION
13. WORLDWIDE VERSION [NEW TESTAMENT
14. THE VOICE
15. THE AMPLIFIED BIBLE
16. NEW LIVING TRANSLATION

FAITH

Faith is the assurance that whatever we hope for and believe we will receive or get it.

The Seventh-Sense Faith begins with this mindset: Whatever you vividly conceive or imagine and hope for, passionately long for or desire, courageously believe and repeatedly ask for, painstakingly and sacrificially pursue, enthusiastically and actively work on, patiently and committedly wait for will surely manifest or materialize in its physical equivalence.

CONTENTS

ACKNOWLEDGEMENT

My thanks go to Ed Vasquez whose persistence during negotiations convinced me to have this book published by AuthorHouse publishers. He has endeared himself to my heart and so he has a space in this book.

I will always remember my children Eziuche and Chidinma whose love inspired me. My prayer is that they will remain faithful to the end. Many thanks to my friend Natalie Rosemary Scott, who helped me in many ways in the process of completing this book get.

Finally I pray for special blessings on all who will read this book: that your faith would be strengthened and that your Seventh-Sense would become your strongest weapon even in your weakest moments.

PREFACE

In the history of the world there was never a public revelation of the seventh sense until Jesus Christ; and among the early apostles and disciples none else understood and utilized faith consciously and intentionally as the Apostle Paul who wrote extensively about it in his Pauline epistles.

Yet faith was not revealed to him as the seventh sense. Today God is making a conscious effort to reveal faith to the world as your seventh, most powerful and highest sense-ability ever known to man. With faith you will conquer and overcome any and every obstacle and rise above life's inhibiting factors, self limiting beliefs, thoughts and mind set; particularly spiritual and supernatural factors that so easily beset us and master us.

The seventh sense is the new revelation that the media should pick up and publicize for the benefit of all mankind. Therefore, everyone should understand that faith is not a religious word but a living word and a human word. We should talk about it in the public, teach it to our children in schools, and study it in the universities. It holds the key to solving most of humanities problems, eradicating poverty, creating superabundance, solving conflict and restoring peace to the world. Faith is peaceful and works well in the atmosphere of peace. A well developed money-sense is not picked up on the street so also faith-sense or seventh sense knowledge is not picked in the street. It must be taught even from childhood.

Once in a century God releases wisdom to access His divine nature and attributes and illuminates human minds to understand some mysteries of creation or that exist in creation which have not been revealed before. The seventh sense is one of such mysteries. I must confess that I do not understand this reality anymore than any one else but it's been revealed for us to study and research its validity.

We all understand the five senses and some people understand the sixth sense but the seventh sense is still a mystery. Due to this ignorance we all use the seventh sense everyday and in different ways but do not know or understand and recognize it. This ignorance has led to the sub-functioning and underutilization and under-development of faith in our lives.

One aspect of faith that we are familiar with is obviously faith toward God. But there is also faith toward self, other people and toward things. The seventh sense controls and harnesses all the abilities of all the other senses and empowers then to their highest state of fitness, achievement and capabilities that we allow.

Each sense instrument performs a specific role. For instance, the eye is for seeing and visioning, the ear is for hearing and auditory but the seventh sense, faith, is for empowerment and surfing the wonderful and limitless worlds of the unknown where everything is possible.

Faith empowers imagination, action, visioning, risk-taking, personal development, success, achievement and life itself. It is the consummation and the realization of everything we are and everything we need and hope to become. Faith is such a beautiful spiritual and emotional sense that makes everything possible.

Because faith is a Spirit 'the spirit if faith', we must believe it before we can access it. Anything short of believing is academic and terrestrial. The scripture says "And since we have the same spirit of faith, according to what is written, "I believed and therefore I spoke," we also believe and therefore speak." 2 Corinthians 4:13.

Therefore, if you do not believe then you should not speak or criticize this assertion because you are not standing on the same pedestal as those who believe. You have to be a believer in order to fully understand the spiritual aspects of faith. As I said earlier, faith is both a spiritual and a natural word.

As the eye is specialized purely for seeing or visioning, the ear solely for hearing and the hand purposely for handling, touching or holding, so also is faith designed for enhancement, activation and empowerment of all the other senses. Because the seventh sense is not physical as the five senses it possesses supernatural sense-abilities of its own and, therefore, can and do override the physical senses in the exercise of its role. For instance, a blind man cannot see with the physical eyes but a blind man can have faith and see with the seventh sense.

FAITH AND FULFILMENT

Earl Nightingale said, "We are at our very best, and we are happiest, when we are fully engaged in the work we enjoy on the journey toward the goal we've established for ourselves. It gives meaning to our pursuit and comfort to our sleep. It makes everything else in life wonderful and so worthwhile."

In the same vein I also say.., We are at our very best, and we are happiest when we totally engage our Seventh- Sense toward the realization of the goals and dreams that we have set for ourselves. It gives purpose and assurance to our efforts and peace of mind to our souls. It makes life worthwhile, worth living, wonderful and fulfilled. It is only through faith that we can transcend our limitations.

This is because you can see farer afield with the eyes of faith, hear and understand the inaudible, touch and take hold of the realms of the supernatural and lift up ourselves from our limiting factors. The seventh sense is a sense worth developing because your life will be accelerating at your highest level of both divine and human vibration.

You may not be totally fulfilled when you are not living in the level of your highest faith. There will still continue to be the void and emptiness that constantly yawns to be filled. It is at the level of your seventh sense or highest faith that you are fulfilled and at peace with yourself. When you are at peace with yourself, almost everything else will be at peace with you and you will find fulfilment in whatever you do whether you are rich or poor it doesn't matter. Life does not necessarily consist in the abundance of things you possess but in the quality of faith-power you command.

Listen to Apostle Paul's valedictory message about the fulfilment of life's purpose. "I have fought the good fight,

I have finished the race, I have kept the faith. Now there is in store for me the crown of righteousness, which the Lord, the righteous Judge, will award to me on that day—and not only to me, but also to all who have longed for his appearing." 2Timothy 4:7-8.

FAITH AND LIFE

The Seventh Sense supports and enriches life, hope, joy, patience, wholeness, peace, love, supernatural illumination and divine nature. The reason most Christians have not attained the level of oneness with God that they desire is because of our shallow understanding of faith and the lack of conscious and intentional application of the power of our seventh sense.

It is written "God is faithful" and Jesus lamented the lack of faith in his disciples and in his generation. If God himself uses faith to operate, how is it that we have become to big and too scientific that we count faith irrelevant in our lives today? Yes, whether you realize it now or not you need faith to operate successfully in this world no matter your level of your education or the lack thereof. Faith is one of the most essentials of life just as money is the most essential for living. Faith is not gotten through much education, in fact, the opposite has proved to be the norm, i.e. the more educated and rich the less we think of faith. Yet when the more educated find faith, they seem to abandon everything else in pursuit of the uplifting and fulfilling power of the seventh sense.

As said before all achievements and successes come from the application of faith, it follows, therefore, that to enjoy success, joy, peace, good health, abundance, wholeness/wellness and a higher than normal quality of life on a continual basis, you must understand and apply faith principles. It is not very difficult but requires a new orientation and practice.

The word faith has become so synonymous with religion and religious jargon that it is fast losing its meaning. Seeing faith only in the light of religion is dangerous and makes people shy away from the real meaning and importance of the word and its concepts, implications and applications towards its actual purpose[s]. Faith is much higher and deeper than the cursory definitions attached to it.

Faith is actually your Seventh Sense [7th Sense]. Faith is a perceptive-sensory power within you. It is higher and more powerful than all the other six senses combined and is completely within your control. It is high time we took a more serious look at this powerful and unique sense-ability that is freely given to us and which many of us have very little understanding of.

Faith is not just a religious word. It is a success button. It is the undiscovered, under-developed and underutilized sense-ability that will change your world if you tap into it and develop it as any one of the other senses. The other six senses are sight, touch, smell, taste, hearing and the unnatural/supernatural faculty of the sixth sense which I call the super-conscious. The super-conscious, to a large extent, involuntarily accesses the supernatural world without the conscious efforts of the individual and that includes miracles. Faith is higher than miraculous manifestations because faith was before miracles and faith produces miraculous manifestations and not the other way around.

Faith on the other hand accesses the invisible worlds with all consciousness and can be developed, controlled and utilized at will to give and/or receive things from the supernatural and invisible worlds particularly from God. Although the word faith is used mostly in religious circles and I have used it in line with scriptures in this book; faith is a human word that makes things to happen in the natural world that would not have otherwise. Because much of what we know about faith comes from the scriptures, many people think the word is purely a religious word. Faith works from within you to harness and connect the God of all creation. Do you have faith, if you do, in what or who? Faith is the hand that receives gifts and blessings from the Omnipotent. Faith is your success button.

INTRODUCTION

Do you know that you have more senses than five? Have you heard that you have the sixth and seventh senses? Do you know anything about your seventh sense? Do you know that the seventh sense motivates and to a large measure controls all the other senses? Would you like to know more about this powerful and super-ordinary sense? Would you like to know how your success and failure in life and eternity could depend on how you use your seventh sense? This book will bring you into reality with your most valuable perceptive, sensory and spiritual gift.

Furthermore, have you ever wondered why you are sometimes or so often afraid, and have you thought of why you sometimes find it difficult to take decisions or make up your mind quickly even when you have all the information you need? Are you surprised about your inability to take firm action on some issues and on other issues you take strong and immediate action? And have you considered why you are so risk averse or afraid to take risks? These and more questions will be discussed in the chapters that follow. This book, the Amazing Power of Faith, will bring you to a new realm of power and possibilities that will change your life now and for all eternity.

Faith is your Seventh Sense. Faith is the most amazing force or power that resides within you. Faith is a universal phenomenon. Everyone possesses a measure of it. Everyone uses it to some extent. Everyone needs more of it. Everyone falls short of accessing the full power and potentials of faith as a sense instrument.

As a sense instrument, faith harnesses all the qualities of the other six senses, so that it can see, hear, smell, touch, walk, talk, and perceive just like them. And it also has force, speed, power and abilities far beyond our human comprehension. Faith is a naturally spiritual grace or gift that you were born with; it develops and grows as you grow older until it peaks at a certain age or until you renew or activate the spiritual faith. Faith as the Seventh-Sense is the undiscovered, underutilized and underestimated perceptive/ sensory instrument or ability in human existence.

Faith is the conviction or confidence that helps us to believe things, make decisions, take actions and take risks. Faith is the force or power that motivates from within. Faith, like grace, permeates every fabric of our being and affects every aspect of our lives. You could never live a day without faith.

Faith will make you rise to any occasion or challenging situations without fear. Faith is what makes you get off the bed in the morning without even thinking. Faith will lift you to higher realms of being and higher dimensions of achievements and excellence when you truly understand it. A good knowledge of faith and how it works will change you from a wimp to a hero, from a failure to an achiever, from a looser to an overcomer and from a coward to a man/woman of valor, gallantry and vibrancy. Faith will make you the person you always wanted to be.

CHAPTER 1

DEFINITION

What is Faith?

First, faith is a complete acceptance of an idea (truth or false), which cannot be demonstrated or proved by the process of logical, rational and scientific thinking. Faith is the virtue or power within you by which you believe, act and/or hold on to an idea, thought or information without fear or doubt. Faith is a complete acceptance of truth or idea without seeking for evidence or prior proof. Faith is self-conviction, belief, trust and confidence.

Second, faith is also the supernatural power within you or the gateway to the supernatural. Faith is the power that transmutes what you desire into reality. It is the energy or power that harnesses ideas from the spiritual and infinite into physical action or reality.

Faith is a conditioned state of mind that generates power or force that moves invisible objects, obstacles and mountains and lifts one into the realms of the supernatural. Faith is an emotion, a different kind of emotion that connects us to our spiritual roots. Faith generates emotions and certain emotions can generate faith. When faith is mixed with action, feeling, and/or speech, it can produce results far greater than the finite action or words that preceded it. Faith can turn an idea into its physical evidence or reality through proper actions. Faith is the active ingredient in every success or achievement and without faith there will be no manifestations of hope.

Faith is the engine or power that drives hope, actions, optimism, commitment, enthusiasm, loyalty, success, achievement, holiness and other virtues of life. Faith operates mainly in the spiritual realms. It is the power behind the six D's of success: desire, decision, discipline, determination, dedication, and definiteness of purpose. Without these there is no success. In order words, faith is the basic ingredient for the attainment of any kind of success in life; whether academic, financial, spiritual, business, etc. Without faith there is no achievement ever.

Faith is a spirit and a spiritual gift. It is the interface between the physical and the spiritual, the natural and the supernatural. It is the supernatural force that moves and activates all other spiritual gifts and emotions such as love, joy, hope, patience, peace, fruitfulness, healing, miracles, baptism of the Holy Spirit, word of wisdom, discerning of spirits and so on. Faith is the power that energizes and motivates your life.

Faith is the inner strength of your life. It is the power that makes you maintain the momentum of life. The realization of the power of faith within you will change your life forever for the better. You will be accelerating at a higher and stronger vibration of internal energy and positive momentum if you are living by faith. You can do the impossible, see the invisible, change the unchangeable, overcome adverse circumstances and situations, receive grace to go through the unthinkable and live a longer, healthier, more contented and fulfilled life.

The power of faith is the power of hope. It is the power within you. It is the power in the mind or the mind power. Faith-power is dependent on the strength and resources of the higher powers backing it. Faith without a backbone is empty and presumptuous. For instance, if what you base your faith on is a carved wood, stone, metal or any other works of men's hands, it will fail you. Faith is not based on visible things or empty creeds, chants, persons, self or some religious jargons and superfluities. Those will disappoint you.

Faith emanates from a Supreme Being who is full of faith. His goings, His words and His actions are full of faith.

No one can approach, understand or interact with Him through any other means except through faith. In the realm of faith, He is as real as any man in the physical realm. Faith is based on the living knowledge of this Infinite-One, the Omnipotent, Omnipresent, Omniscient and Omni-wealthy*. He is the Maker, Creator, Sustainer and Owner of the universe. I call Him the One and only Faith-full God.

Faith will sustain you for life and at all times and in all places and you will be a success in what ever you do. When I talk about this Faith-full One, I mean the Universal Supreme God of faith who is just, perfect, without injustice and without partiality and without iniquity or sin.

Faith is the power behind every answered prayer and every miracle worked or received. Faith is the power for success and achievement. Faith resides in the spirit and is processed in the mind. Faith works best with prayer, affirmations, definite pursuit or purpose and planned actions. When faith is mixed with strong feelings, definiteness of purpose and planned actions, there is no force on earth that can stop or defeat it. Faith is an attribute of the Divine, a medium of exchange in the spirit realm and the power of engagement both in the physical and supernatural. Faith mixed with action brings visible results. Faith is the energy that works within.

---

*   Omni-wealthy - a word coined by the author

CHAPTER 2

TWO TYPES OF FAITH

There are two kinds of faith: Natural and Spiritual. The natural faith is the kind of faith that comes naturally to you from birth and operates naturally in normal situations. It is inherited as a natural grace. Natural faith helps you believe and trust other humans or people. This trust enhances interactions and socializations in normal daily situations. Natural faith allows you to step out of bed in the morning, believe that your car will start when you turn on the ignition or that the light will turn on when you flip the switch on, etc. These and many more are examples of using your natural finite faith. Natural faith is rooted in our innate abilities of age, physical strength, possessions, wisdom, knowledge, experiences, graces, gifts, your support networks, acquaintances and not necessarily in God. It is what makes humans not live in unnecessary and abnormal fears or phobia as animal and birds.

Spiritual faith on the other hand has to do with God, the Faith-full One. God is a Spirit and the Father of spirits.

Hebrews 12:9 reads "Moreover, we have all had human fathers who disciplined us and we respected them for it. How much more should we submit to the Father of spirits and live?"

Spiritual faith is that kind of faith that is consciously and purposefully activated or induced in order to connect with powers and forces beyond the natural realms. It is the kind of faith you employ when you have exhausted all natural options and have nowhere else or no one else to turn to. Spiritual faith unlike its natural counterpart is rooted in the Infinite and the Invisible. Most times when we talk about faith we mistake our natural faith for the spiritual faith.

The spiritual faith is the creative faith. This creative kind of faith draws from the infinite resources of the Divine and is the source of all unusual, unnatural and creative super-abilities of God. This kind of faith is based in God and can do or change any impossible natural and spiritual circumstance or situation. It works mostly in the spirit realms but the results are manifested both physically and spiritually.

Spiritual faith is very powerful, wonder-working, problem solving, creative and specific. It is not as generic as the natural faith. Everyone does not possess it and it is not inherited. It is a gift, learned, developed, practiced, induced, grown and maintained. Only very few people in all of history have mastered it. It is not at all difficult to acquire but because people are so preoccupied with what they can see, touch, hear, taste and feel with their natural five senses, we do not bother much about what we do not see or know. Many of us do not have the patience and dedication required to grow and sustain spiritual faith. Typically, it requires godliness and in its purest forms, holiness and oneness with the Divine.

Everyone that has achieved or received notable inventions, miraculous powers and other supernatural creative abilities has gone through the avenue or channels of the spiritual faith without exception. Everyone has the innate capacity to attain the heights of spiritual faith. Some people dabble into it by accident but most others by purposeful pursuits. Creative inventors could tap into the creative part of the spiritual faith with or without religiosity. Spiritual faith has many applications but we use it mostly in prayer and affirmations.

Spiritual faith has levels. Everyone is not on the same level and academic achievement does not change the equation. In fact academics could be on the lower levels of faith because some academicians do not like to believe on what cannot be measured, quantified, researched and documented through the five senses of smell, feel, hear, see and taste. Spiritual faith on the other hand is at a higher level that over-rules all the powers of the five senses. Faith is in class seven while some of these other senses and disciplines are in classes one, two or three. For that reason some academic disciplines hate the notion of faith and God because they do not understand it and cannot test and measure God and faith in the laboratories. They extol the power of man and the five senses or they extol the power of demons that inspire some of such academics. Thee Bible declares "But the natural man does not receive (understand) the things of the spirit of God for they are foolishness to him neither can he know them because they are spiritually discerned." 1 Corinthians 2:14.

It is possible that a blind, crippled and illiterate person can exercise a higher level of spiritual faith than a PhD holder in some disciplines that you find academicians who deny the existence of faith and God. The faith-sense or the 7th Sense is by far superior to the other senses in that faith connects the spiritual and the natural, and also because all the other senses derive their power and drive from faith. I am not in any way knocking on academics or literacy but stating the truth about faith. For the purposes of this study, I will use faith to mean spiritual faith unless otherwise stated. The dividing line between the spiritual and natural faith is so thin that one can crisscross them inadvertently.

Faith Exposition

Faith is a process. Whatever you vividly imagine, passionately desire, courageously believe, confidently ask for; painstakingly and sacrificially pursue; actively and enthusiastically hope for and patiently and persistently wait on will surely materialize. This is also the definition of achievement, success, accumulation of wealth, and the pursuit of happiness or holiness. Purpose driven faith can accomplish almost anything. What you do not believe will take time to materialize if ever.

Spiritual faith is as simple as believing in God the Supreme Being and the Infinite Intelligence. He is the possessor and creator of all wisdom, power and wealth. He is full of faith and we are allowed to draw from His faith-fullness. Without this basic belief, you cannot have positive spiritual faith. There is also a negative spiritual side of faith but I warn you to keep away from that because it will put you in bondage and ultimately destroy you. Faith is one but you can apply it for positive or negative purposes.

Harnessing Your Faith

Faith is a process. It is a process of seeing the invisible with your faith or spiritual eyes. It is a process of organizing, directing and pin-pointing your mind: [will, intellect and emotions] to the object of your invisible desire; then harnessing and connecting your conscience [conscious, subconscious and super-conscious], toward obtaining it. And finally it is a process of taking the right action[s] to establish it. The action could be speaking to the situation or praying, making an affirmation or pronouncement and waiting with perseverance and expectation to receive. It could be doing or trying something new that you have never tried before.

Using your faith is the process of packaging your desire into a container called prayer or affirmation and declaring it with confidence to the Supreme Being, the God who has the ultimate power, ability and resource to perform and supply. In His presence prayers are weighed for faith-quality and assurance. This is where your request will be processed for merit and turned into its natural or physical equivalence then sent back to you in the form of answered request. Whether the request is for spiritual or natural purposes does not matter.

Faith works best when the mind concentrates totally with undivided attention on the object of your desire without distractions, fear or doubt. Faith sees the end from the beginning and believes in the superabundance of the infinite resources in the beyond. Faith sees, knows and believes what no other senses can comprehend. It is in a realm of its own and operates with absolute leverage over the other senses. For these reasons faith is in a class seven, the highest sensory and perceptive capability class ever known to man.

CHAPTER 3

UNDERSTANDING OF FAITH

Before you can begin to articulate spiritual faith you must first believe that there is a Supreme Being over and above all; God. Hebrews 11: 6 declares "And without faith it is impossible to please (find) God, because anyone who comes to him must believe that he exists and that he rewards those who earnestly seek him." Without this first principle of faith, you can never have a positive spiritual faith. This is because faith is based on the reality of the invisible realms of the Supreme Being, God. The first principle of faith is believing or belief. The second is acting [on what you believe]. The third is hoping. The fourth is patience [waiting]. The fifth is expectation [active expectation].

God is [a] Spirit. God is also a personality, a spiritual person if you will. God is invisible as all spirits are. Spiritual faith is the farthermost extension of the natural faith. Everyone has the natural faith to believe in other people through their words, works or witnesses from other people. We even believe those we have never met before because of what we have heard about them. Those people are invisible to us yet we belief that they exist because of the testimonies of others.

Furthermore, most people believe in the concept of ghosts and spirits that they do exist. If you believe that ghosts exist, whether the ghosts of dead people or evil spirits and angels, then you already have a partial knowledge of the Invisible Father of spirits. Spirits are also creations or children of God the Father of spirits. Where there are children, there must of necessity be a father. Those who have problems believing in one Supreme Being, God, but believe in ghosts and spirits do thereby exhibit their spiritual ignorance or direct rebelliousness to the Father of spirits and, therefore, condemn themselves to eternal death and punishment by willful disobedience and rebellion. God is also the judge of the whole earth.

If, however, we believe that there are [invisible] spirits and ghosts and we say that we do not believe in the existence of God the Father of spirits, who is deceiving who and aren't we deluding ourselves? So also by extension you can extrapolate that if there are spirits and ghosts there must be a Chief Spirit, a Lead Spirit, a Captain Spirit or a President, King, Lord and Father of spirits.

Furthermore, think for a moment if you believe that spirits can do amazing things such as travel at lightening speed, pass through walls and closed doors, kill or help people, cause havoc and bring good omens, etc., then you already believe in God. You may, however, refuse to or become stubborn and disobedient as some of the spirits (evil spirits) were also rebellious to God the Father of spirits in the past. Your faith or unbelief does not change God nor the fact that there is a Universal Supreme Being the English calls God. I don't know what He is called in your own language but I am sure He has a name in your own language too.

However, if you do not believe, you are short changing your faith and your ability to connect with this awesome Being who has the ability and capability to help you to the utmost. The scripture declares in Hebrews 7:25 Amplified Version. Therefore, He is able also to save to the uttermost [completely, perfectly, finally, and for all time and eternity] those who come to God through Him [Christ], since He is always living to make petition to God and intercede with Him and intervene for them.

Just as some children can be disobedient to their parent so also can parents and adults be disobedient to their Heavenly Spiritual Father. In fact adults are more rebellious and disobedient to God their Father than do children to their earthly parents. Most children do things out of ignorance but adults out of deliberate desire to rebel because they think or want to believe that there is no one else above them to be answerable to. This is a delusion of the worst order. Every one is answerable to God whether we like it or not and whether we want to believe it now or later. The truth is that we will believe it someday soon. Be it here on earth or in eternity somewhere beyond.

Think for a moment how you feel when your own children are disobedient or rebellious to you and imagine how God feels when you as an adult are rebellious and disobedient to him. How would you feel if your own children refuse to believe whatever you tell them, doubt and question every word you speak, tell people openly that you are a liar and that you are not their father but an impersonator or impostor.

How would you feel when your beloved child the one you love most turns against you and actually oppose you to your face and make others to disbelieve, oppose, challenge, insult your dignity, align with your mortal enemy to fight and oppose you. Do you know that is actually what we do to God when we say that there is no God and go about saying and doing all sorts of things that insult, and anger Him? If you've been doing all or some of those things, it is time to turn to and repent and believe God. "If we confess our sins, He is faithful and just to forgive us our sins and to cleanse us from all unrighteousness." 1John 1:9. God exist and is really very close to you, even closer than you can ever imagine. You can say this short prayer with me.

Dear God, I never really knew how to find you and so thought that you really do not exist. Now I know better. Please forgive me of all my disobedience and rebellion against you. I do believe in you now and henceforth will seek to know you better all the days of my life. Thank you for opening my understanding and bringing me to this realization now. I thank you Jesus. Amen.

Having said that prayer you are now ready to start the journey of spiritual faith. Because you now understand some spiritual truths and principles, you are now in a position to activate your spiritual faith. The Scripture says "Now faith is the substance of things hoped for, the evidence of things not seen." Hebrews 11:1. Everything we need and can image already exists in the spirit world. That is the reason new things that people imagine do manifest themselves in the world everyday both great and small. It depends on how you think and the size of our faith. The bigger your thoughts and imaginations, the higher your faith to accomplish them will be. God will always honor faith wherever He finds it. Faith is not found in religions or in religious activities and chants. Faith is not just a religious word; it is the energy of life. Faith is resident in all people including children of God who trust Him completely and absolutely.

The God of faith is a Universal God. He is neither a Christian, Jew, Muslim, Hindu, Buddha, Sikh, Confucius nor a founder of any other religion for that matter. He is the God of the whole earth. He is the God of all those who believe in Him through faith in Jesus Christ. He is the God of those who put their trust in Him. Spiritual faith proceeds from Him alone and any one who receives the gift of faith is a believer because it comes from God Almighty alone. There is no religion in heaven. There are only believers in the Faith-full God.

Faith and Belief

Believe means to accept a fact or idea without doubt or reservation. Faith is the application of what you believe. Faith is to act on what you believe without doubt or double minds. Spiritual faith grows from the knowledge of God and knowing God comes from knowing the Word of God. God wants us to know and believe his Word without doubt or reservation. Jesus said to him, "Thomas, because you have seen Me, you have believed. Blessed are those who have not seen and yet have believed." John 20:21. Those who believe are blessed. "And blessed is she that believed: for there shall be a performance of those things which were told her from the Lord." Luke 1:45.

The days of sacrifices to appease or please God are over. God wants us now to believe His Word and trust Him to bring it to pass. God is His Word and God is in His Word to fulfill it. It is the unwavering belief in the Word of God that brings faith. We cannot see God with the naked eyes but we can see, hear, touch and enjoy His presence through faith and with the 7th Sense. Do you believe and act on the Word of God without doubting? If your answer is yes then you may already possess the 7th Sense and a candidate of all divine possibilities. But if your answer is no, but you would want to know more, you may contact this writer or find a Bible believing Pentecostal minister or believer to help you further. Your miracle is very close at hand. However, if your answer is no not now or I'm not ready, remember that life is too short to procrastinate.

CHAPTER 4

SIXTH AND SEVENTH SENSES

The sixth and the seventh senses work in perfect harmony to bring about the desired result of your faith. The sixth sense is an unnatural and unusual sense of perception-ability into the unseen realms of the supernatural. To claim to have or use the sixth sense you should be able to use it at will which most people cannot lay claims to. Furthermore, most people who claim to use the sixth sense do not have control over what they perceive.

When you do things instinctively or intuitively you might be using or experiencing some measure of your sixth sense in action. Moreover, those who actually use and rely only on the sixth sense may be ranked low on faith because they rely more on perception and their spirit guide. This book is not about the sixth sense; therefore, we will not delve deeply into that subject. There are ample resources on the subject. The sixth sense makes use of the subconscious and the super-conscious abilities of the mind to access the supernatural realms and the person using it might not have much control over what he/she does or perceives. People sometimes see things, hear voices/noises, smell fragrances, sleep- walk, etc., using their sixth sense but are never in complete control.

The 7th Sense on the other hand is within your reach and control. You can access it at all times even in your dreams and the results can be visible, quantifiable and documentable as in the case of miracles, inventions, salvation, baptism of the holy spirit, healings, deliverances, etc. All other senses can be and are activated through faith. The 7th Sense harnesses and makes use of spiritual faith-ability or faith-power.

Faith-The Seventh Sense

Faith is the seventh sensory-perceptive ability after the normal five senses and the sixth sense which is your enhanced, unnatural, perception-ability into things in the unseen worlds. Faith as a sensory ability supersedes all the others in that it has all the other senses of its own.

Faith is the compass of the soul. As the airplane cannot go very far without a compass, so we would not be able to effectively and successful navigate the trouble water of life without a well developed sense of faith. The airplane can travel round the world without eyes but with a compass can find its destination and locate the runway. So can a believer with a well developed faith-sense.

Faith as the 7th Sense has eyes and can see. This is called the eyes of faith. It has ears and can hear. This is the ears of faith. It has hands and can reach out and touch. This is the arms of faith. It has voice that can speak. This is the word of faith. It has feet or legs and can walk/ move. This is the walk of faith. It has its own power. This is the power of faith. "Now to Him who is able to do exceedingly abundantly above all that we ask or think, according to the power that works in us." Ephesians 3:20. The power that works in us in this context is the power of faith or the power of God. Faith power is God's power. Faith has resources at its disposal. These are the gifts of faith. Faith always has a song. This is the song of victory. The bible says "…and this is victory that overcomes the world – even our faith." IJohn 5:4. The lyrics of a song say: "We are more than conquerors, overcomers in this world. We have been made victorious through the blood of Jesus Christ."

Faith will work in, with and through all the other senses to accomplish purposes, dreams and desires. Jesus said if you have faith as small as a mustard seed you can move (spiritual) mountains. Matthew 17:20. Faith is the power within you to move mountains, do the impossible and achieve the inconceivable. One may ask me are you there yet? No, not yet but growing.

Faith as the 7th Sense is very little known of. That may explain why many people especially Christians are so stunted in spiritual growth. I am not writing as one who has achieved or know any better than anybody else. I am writing according to the grace of revelation given to me. I have been struggling with my own faith up till now. As you read this book and learn, so I write and learn too. This book is for a new generation of people especially believers who want to live in the atmosphere of the supernatural and take the leap-of-faith and harness their God given 7th Sense and excel. This book is a call to believers to do more research on the 7th Sense. Faith is real power but works well with prayers, sound knowledge of the Word and directed actions.

Without the active use of your 7th Sense, you may not be able to access the rich storehouse of God at will. Faith is a divine attribute of the Almighty and the medium of exchange between God and man. It is now incumbent on us to learn how to use this precious gift of life upon which our destinies depend to a large extent. Your 7th Sense is your gateway to success, prosperity, peace, joy, healings, deliverance, miracles and the supernatural. God requires us to activate and use our faith. In fact no communication can take place between you and God if you do not approach or come to Him by faith. "And without faith it is impossible to please God, because anyone who comes to him must believe that he exists and that he rewards those who earnestly seek him." Hebrews 11:6. We limit the Holy One and what He can do for us and through us because of lack of faith. Without faith it is impossible to give or receive from God.

CHAPTER 5

CATEGORIES OF FAITH

There are different types of faith:

Positive faith
Negative faith
Great faith
Small faith
Godly faith
Ungodly faith
Faithfulness
Faithlessness
Assumed faith
Presumptive faith
True faith
Bold faith
No Faith – Deuteronomy 32: 19; Mark 4:40
Active faith
Passive faith
Vertical faith
Horizontal faith

Measure of faith

I will write only on some of these types of faith.

Positive Faith

Positive faith is that faith that comes with good intentions and purposes. It is the faith with which you accomplish good and worthwhile achievements. It is the faith that is governed and directed by peace of mind, love, joy, justice, fairness, truth and compassion, kindness, humility and other good virtues of life.

When applied, positive faith will goad you into higher realms of life and spirituality. Positive faith affects you and others positively and it is the basis of wellbeing, wholesomeness, sound mind, spiritual uplift, good health, miracles and other forms of blessing. Positive faith can be sustained all life-long through confidence, positive desires, right choices, right decisions and great achievement. Positive faith is the base or ground for all positive achievements and a confident personality. Positive faith is very desirable and must be encouraged in our children and young adults who are not yet fully set in their beliefs. Positive faith should also be encouraged in all adult who are struggling in life. Positive faith will give a good and enviable lifestyle but negative faith will bring you regrets all your life. Positive faith is the good and natural way of faith. It leads to hope, peace, contentment and good life. Faith is a positive energy but can be used with negative intentions. Watch out.

Negative Faith

Negative faith on the other hand is the direct opposite of the positive faith. It is equally as effective and potent as the positive faith. The difference is that it produces negative results of hate, destruction and all sorts of evil work. When it is applied neither you nor the person it is directed toward will experience peace, joy, love or blessing. Negative faith affects everyone involved negatively whether it is an unkind word spoken, anger, evil thoughts and imaginations or wicked acts. Negative faith is very destructive and does nothing good except bring about misery, destruction, anger, frustration, evil, regrets, punishment, hell and damnation.

Negative faith is the faith used by all who commit evil, crime, murder, rape, bullying, racism, inequality, injustice, crime against humanity and satanism, etc. Everyone that commits crime does so out of the application of the negative faith. The subconscious mind does not differentiate between types of faith but acts on the dominant thoughts and imaginations that reaches and affects it. Therefore, it is very possible for you to believe strongly in a negative thing and apply faith as you would a positive things and it becomes a negative faith. You can do this without knowing it is a negative faith. Many of us have done so times without number unknowingly, but the danger is habitually and knowingly living in your negative faith. Un-forgiveness, bitterness, anger, pessimisms and other negative virtues only serve to increase the chances of your living and using your faith negatively. Every negative pronouncement made by faith puts a curse on the recipient. That is an example of the use of a negative faith. The Bible admonishes us to guard our heart with all diligence for out of it flow the forces of life. Proverbs 4:23. "Be careful how you think, your life is shaped by your thoughts." The good thing about negative faith is that it can be changed or transformed into a positive faith. But do not move from positive to negative faith because the result is usually disastrous or catastrophic.

Measure of Faith

Measure of faith talks about the level of faith you have and are operating in at any given time. Because faith is subliminal, it is possible to gain or increase faith and/or lose or lower your faith fairly rapidly. Measures of faith includes: positive faith and negative faith, high faith and low faith, strong faith and weak faith, small faith and great faith, faithlessness and faithfulness; others are godly faith and godless faith, sustainable or unsustainable faith, bold faith, true faith and no faith or cowardice. All these types of faith are descriptions or measures of the types of and levels of faith that people exhibit and operate in.

Faith has levels. Faith is never static. It is either growing or diminishing. You are either gaining or losing faith, getting stronger or growing weaker in faith. Faith loss/gain is a slow process. It will diminish if it is not growing. My admonition is to always seek for growth possibilities for your faith. For faith to continue to be available, it must be maintained and sustained through the process of Faith-awareness and understanding. That is what this book is all about. Purity (of life and conscience) is a major faith booster. Faith grows exponentially with the increase of purity in the heart and with increased intake of the Word of God. A heart corrupted by fear, doubt and sin cannot produce a higher level of faith. Measures of faith help us to know where our faith is and what we are doing to our faith by the things we allow.

Measure of faith is the quality and not the quantity of faith that you give in exchange for what you are asking or what you need. It is the measure of the amount of pure-faith that you produce and provide for your need. The greater and purer the faith, the more effective it is in bringing the desired result. Measure of faith assesses and appraises the quality of your present faith not past faith. It could be possible that a preacher healed a dead man and brought him back to life five years ago but is unable to heal headaches today because his present level of pure faith has diminished greatly within the last two years. This does not mean that the power to heal resides in the preacher. It means rather that the faith to receive has diminished.

Present faith is the quality of your pure faith at the time of praying or application of faith in exchange for your need. Faith as we have said earlier is the medium of exchange in the spirit realms. In order words, faith is the money or currency of the spirit worlds. It stands to reason, therefore, that some of the richest people in this world could be some of the poorest in the spiritual realms because of their devotion and dependence on the currencies of this world and vice versa. That was why Jesus said "And again I say unto you, it is easier for a camel to go through the eye of a needle, than for a rich man to enter into the kingdom of God." Matthew 19:24. For the same reason also, many poor people who do not have faith in God will find it difficult to access the divine riches which are obtained through faith in God.

Present faith is what you need to access God's divine riches. There is nothing like a future faith. Faith is now. Hope is for a later time. Let us work on our present faith to purify it so that it can be effective against the enemies of our souls and the distractions of faith written in a future chapter. Past faith is the faith of yesterday. Past faith cannot apply today but the knowledge of it can help you grow your present faith.

Pure-faith is the amount of concentrated, unadulterated and purified faith that a believer produces or presents during prayer for and in exchange for what he or she needs. Pure faith is the highest form of faith, the kind of faith that pleases God. "And without faith it is impossible to please God, because anyone who comes to him must believe that he exists and that he rewards those who earnestly seek him." Hebrews 11:6. Pure faith is the kind of faith that Jesus was alluding to in Luke 17:6. NIV. "He replied, "If you have faith as small as a mustard seed, you can say to this mulberry tree, 'Be uprooted and planted in the sea,' and it will obey you. Do not seek to have much faith rather seek to have pure and practical faith. Faith that is not practical is not pure faith. It is called quantum- faith [quantity of faith].

Assumption Faith

Assumption-faith is a wrong faith and that is surprisingly what many people have. Any faith that is based alone on self or any other terrestrial will last only for a while and when the trial of faith and the vicissitudes of life come, fear overruns them. Fear is by far the worst enemy of man and it has no regard to your present status or financial accumulations. Fear can manifest itself through ill health, financial losses, job loss or joblessness, business losses, loss of a loved one and a host of other ways. For that reason you need an anchor that is much bigger than you and that cannot fail or falter when your faith is tried.

Do not ever rest your faith on your current status; that is pride. Scripture declares, "Pride goes before destruction, and a haughty spirit before a fall." Proverbs 16: 18. Pride always falls and disgracefully fails. Faith, active faith in God will never fail you. This is an assurance and a guarantee. Let us learn some lessons from men like Adolf Hitler, Saddam Hussein, Muammar al-Quaddafi, Idi Amin and a host of others such people as Nebuchadnezzar, Pharaoh among those of the ancient history, etc. The scripture says "Have faith in God" Mark 11:22.

Faith is the energy that runs our lives just as gasoline is the fuel that runs our cars. Your spiritual life cannot run properly without adequate positive faith. Your faith is your spiritual energy. Like your thought, faith is one thing that you alone have absolute control over. You can use it any way you want.

No Faith

And he said unto them, Why are ye so fearful? how is it that ye have no faith? Mark 4:40.

The phrase No-faith does not mean a complete absence of any faith at all. It only means the absence of faith in a particular person or thing. Everyone has a measure of faith but if you do not put it into any particular pursuit, then you do not have faith in anything. For instance, someone may say I don't believe in God, that does not mean he does not have a natural faith at all, it means he has chosen not to trust God and put his faith in Him. But he does have faith to trust himself, his wealth and maybe Satan. However, since we know that man is as unstable as water, money is a passing vanity and Satan is full of evil works, why would you risk your life in such gambles? No-faith manifests in such statements as, I don't believe you, I don't believe that. I can't, etc. Every time we say I can't, we are limiting our faith and ability to perform to full capacity. Do you have faith or no-faith? Do you want to be a man or woman of faith? Then start to develop your faith immediately and allow your seventh-sense take root and grow.

No faith means you have no faith at all to try. Little faith means you have not enough faith to carry through what you have started. "And immediately Jesus stretched out His hand

and caught him, and said to him, O you of little faith, why did you doubt?" Matthew 14: 31. Great faith means you have faith enough to trust God even when all physical evidences around you are contrary because they could not see the invisible. "Then Jesus answered and said to her, "O woman, great is your faith! Let it be to you as you desire." And her daughter was healed from that very hour." Matthew 15:28.

Jesus said, "Now if God so clothes the grass of the field, which today is, and tomorrow is thrown into the oven, will He not much more clothe you, O you of little faith?" [Matthew 6:30]. Jesus was not saying, "You have no faith." Rather, He was asking, "Why do you have so little faith?"

Stubborn Faith

Stubborn faith is the faith that refuses to quit or give up on a project that is not succeeding at first. However, not every project will succeed for many reasons; but there are many successful projects that started off poorly and then succeeded after many failed attempts or slow start up. A faith project is a project that is conceived inside of you and not just following an order. Faith project is the project of your mind not necessarily from another's. Your faith must be consistent with your words and actions. Even when someone else gives you a project, until you assume it as a personal project and apply your own faith, it is still not your faith project.

You can not say I have a stubborn faith and your belief system and actions do not match what you say or confess and vise versa. Your words, your actions and your faith must line up and be in perfect harmony and agreement all the time. There should be no contradiction in the application on faith. Any contradiction between words and actions immediately and ultimately nullifies your faith. You cannot have faith and be worrying at the same time. No, faith does not work that way. I have had people say "I can't help it" or "I can't help myself", "I am afraid, it's too late", etc. These are all contradictions of faith.

Stubborn faith does not take a 'No', for an answer, but is willing to wait for as long as it takes, does not entertain discouragements, does not make friends with losers, does not go organizing its own pity parties, and does not associate itself deeply with failure. Stubborn faith sees failure as a temporary set back and another opportunity to try or begin again, a time to reassess the last strategy, opportunity to draw nearer to God for help.

Stubborn faith does not cry after a spilled milk or stand at the brink of the red sea and wail. It must find another way. There is always another way, another opportunity.

God is always the God of second chances; notice that I did not say 'a second chance' but second chances. Stubborn faith believes that God will make a way where there is no way. Stubborn faith is deaf to what people say and blind to opinion polls. Stubborn faith does not give up easily especially if it has a word from God. It clears and clarifies things from God before concluding.

Stubborn faith is persistent, consistent, rugged and dogged, prayerful, super-optimistic and expectant. It is renewed and refreshed everyday. Stubborn faith understands that faith expires as soon as it is applied and must be renewed everyday. It understands that 'the downfall of a man is not the end of his life.' Therefore, he gets up as soon as he falls. It understands that life is not always a bed of roses and that there will be good days and bad days, winter and summer, cold and heat. Stubborn faith does not compare itself with others, rather it aims at achieving its own set objectives and goals and to fulfill its own destiny not another's.

CHAPTER 6

FACTS CONERNING FAITH

Faith is the undiscovered power within you. Your faith is your spiritual authority and confidence and the basis of a vibrant but humble personality. Faith is not proud or arrogant. The truth is, everybody has a measure of faith that he/she is born with or inherited at birth. This faith allows children to receive what they desire even when they do not have any capacity to ask and to procure things by and for themselves. This is called natural faith. Natural faith in children is anchored on their parents and guardians abilities, but as they continue to develop, their Faith-tank will continue to depreciate.

As children begin to mature into adolescence their natural faith-tank continues to diminish until there is a serious faith deficit. This becomes first noticeable in the early teens as they begin to gain independence from strict parental control and venture into the independent world of adulthood. It will continue to decrease until it reaches a crisis point at which time he/she must find the Creator to replenish his faith tank. Or else, he will try to become a creator to himself and find ways to fill his faith tank with work, activities, sports, religion, gangsterism, military service, or he tries drugs, sex, stubbornness, and rebellion, etc. If he finds spiritual help, his life will be stabilized. However, if in the early adult life all the foregoing fails to sustain or bring answers to his questing spirit, then he may turn his search to faith in parents, peers, governments, educational pursuits, corporate achievement, sports, drug, alcohol, sexual excesses, self righteousness, etc.

When these also fail he may begin to peer into the unknown worlds of spiritism, occultism, gangsterism and other forms of Satanism or negative-faith. Incidentally the world of Satanism is so very wide and deep that anybody can be deceived into accepting false religion and witchcraft as forms of true religion and godliness especially if it offers power and protection. The sad thing about the ungodly religion is that it does not satisfy the quest for a Godly connection, even though it has the semblance of true faith. Many have been brought into satanic bondages which at first felt like they have found the real thing.

However, sooner or later, they discover that they have been deceived and the search continues until they find grace in Christ. In adulthood there is frantic effort by all to find spiritual faith or Godly-faith but spiritual faith comes only from God the Creator, the Holy One. If a person is able to find and connect with the true God, his life is stabilized and he finds peace, joy and faith from within instead of from the outside as the creator fills up his faith-tank once again. If not the search continues but now with doubts, fears, apprehensions, rationalizations and loss of faith in the true God.

Different people find the creative faith of God and connect to the Infinite Intelligence and through that find peace and creativity. The creative faith of God is in His Word. "In the beginning [before all time] was the Word [Christ], and the Word was with God, and the Word was God Himself. He was present originally with God. All things were made *and* came into existence through Him; and without Him was not even one thing made that has come into being. In Him was Life, and the Life was the Light of men." John 1:1-3.

Most people through purposeful seeking find their true faith in Christ and their life of spiritual faith begins. Sadly though, most of the people who find spiritual faith stop their search and faith development almost immediately because of the overwhelming peace, joy and contentment that follow this experience. Others develop what I call Horizontal Faith instead of Vertical God-Faith. Horizontal God-faith majors in learning, teaching, preaching, praying, worshipping, works and other church activities, all of which are good but they are high in natural faith content than in vertical spiritual-faith content. They build up quantum-faith instead of active.

On the other hand, vertical God-faith reaches higher [vertically] toward God in search, research and especially in the application of creative faith or the creative elements in the new faith they have found. God is a creator and faith in Him restores and reinstalls the creative nature of God in man. The people who use their vertical creative faith excel in power, anointing, creativity, industry and business.

For the same reason some of those who receive the vertical satanic faith also excel in creativity but mainly in negative and destructive things. Those who could not find their ways back to God might end up in untimely death, loss of possessions and all they got from Satan or in and out of troubles throughout life. They could also become terminally or incurably ill or worse. Satan does not give anything for free. The Creator is the only one who gives life and gifts without strings attached. God's gifts are without reproach or repentance. Roman 11:29. However, when a true and godly connection is made with God, faith as the 7th Sense is born and there is no limit to what a person could achieve in the physical and spiritual realms by faith if they pursue the vertical faith.

How Faith Comes

Faith comes, faith grows, faith diminishes and faith dies. Faith is the only avenue by which the supernatural powers of the Divine can be harnessed, developed and accessed at will. There are three ways by which faith comes and grows and works. First faith comes by hearing. In the Bible book of Romans it says "Faith comes by hearing..."[5], but spiritual faith comes only by hearing the Word of God. Roman 10:17.

Second, faith grows by self-suggestions or self-inducement. This is done by deliberately sowing or planting a thought, idea or scripture into you mind and nurturing it by repetition until it takes root and you begin to believe it. Third, faith works through prayer, commands/affirmation and actions. Faith believes in an invisible Supreme Being, God. Unlike all the other senses, faith deals with the invisible and the ethereal. When you believe there is God, then you should not have problem believing in Jesus Christ or angels, etc. If you do have problem, I will encourage you to reexamine your faith in the light of the scriptures or the Word of God beginning from the book of the Gospel of John.

How Faith Grows

Faith grows by repetition and practice. We have heard the cliché, "Practice makes perfect." Practice increases our knowledge, activates and accentuates our auto-response systems and increases our faith or belief in our ability to ask, say, do or receive what we want. For example praying constantly and regularly for a particular thing over a period of time will boast your faith and confidence. With confidence comes assurance and assurance is the seed of faith that opens the floodgate of divine resources and supply. As you receive answers to your prayer, your faith is established and begins to grow.

Faith is never static. It must grow or it might begin to diminish. Practice of faith requires reading, hearing, acting and obeying the Word. Faith also grows through patience, persistence and perseverance. Faith is patient. Faith also grows through trials of faith. Waiting patiently after we have prayed helps to grow your faith and allows you to see the result and also manifestation of our faith.

Faith works by application. Even if you have such great faith that can move mountains and you do not apply it to the required situation you will see no results. This is the problem with many Christians who know and even teach faith like me but when trials of faith come we fail because we do not apply our faith to meet the challenges. Faith does not require a huge amount of words or education to work. It requires simply doing or saying what needs to be done or said at the right time under Divine guidance and grace.

Yes We Can

Years ago, one presidential candidate in the US presidential election in 2008 popularized this maxim, YES WE CAN. He so believed in it that he would chant it in almost every election speech he gave until his supporters believed it and even his opponents also believed. He chanted it so much that almost everyone following his campaign trail believed it. He would chant it with such assurance that almost everyone including his enemies knew that he could win that election; and guess what? He won with a landslide victory. What perhaps he might or might not have known at the time was that he was acting out his faith. But I believed he knew what he was doing. He was giving voice to his faith. He was speaking out what he saw with the eyes of his faith, heard with the ears of his faith and received with the hands of his faith before it ever materialized. That man was Barack Obama, President of the United States of America.

His faith in himself and his God trounced all his limitations and inadequacies to snatch victory from the mouth of the gods, not once but twice. Perhaps we all can learn a lesson from Mr. Obama's political faith. Faith is "whatever you vividly imagine, passionately desire, courageously believe, repeatedly ask for, painstakingly and sacrificially pursue, enthusiastically and actively work on and patiently wait for will surely come to you or materialize."

How to Make Your Faith Work for You

Your faith can only work for you if you put it to work, if you apply it to the situation and if you continue to do it till it becomes a routine part of you. The scripture says "… faith without works is dead." Faith does work. Faith is a doing word, an active word/work. On the other hand, work without faith is legalism or self-righteousness. Faith and action are two sides of the same coin. Believing precedes acting and not acting before believing; but action must follow your belief. Faith, hope and action are the eternal trio that brings our desires and wishes to physical reality.

There is a powerful creative ability or power within the spoken word [your spoken word]. Each word, including careless ones that we speak carries the creative abilities of a god. Scripture says, "…You are gods; and all of you are children of the Most High." Psalm 82:6. Our words have the ability to create what we want or desire if we believe what we say. I once heard of a woman who out of anger said to her troublesome child "may you purge to death" and almost immediately the child started to stool uncontrollably. Words spoken or mixed with the emotions of faith, anger, deep love or any other emotions have the ability to manifest exactly or exceedingly. For that reason, directed and emotionalized words and actions receive immediate answers. The same goes for prayers that are mixed with the emotion of faith, love and expectations.

Commands

Commands are powerful ways to pray. Your faith is your spiritual authority not your position in the church. To pray with faith is praying with authority. Praying with commands emotionalizes your prayer and releases your faith-authority to activate the supernatural to act on your words. Faith-full commands, not empty words, challenge your problems or obstacles and make them to crackle and move or give way. Directed and emotionalized prayer-command destroys the powers that oppose; be they physical or spiritual. For this reason, commands are always obeyed both in the spirit world and in the natural. Even a child can stop an adult with a word of command. So it is also in the spirit realm.

Anchor of Faith

What is an anchor? According to Webster New World Collegiate Dictionary, "An anchor is a heavy object, usually a shaped iron weight with flukes, a devise that holds something else secure." An anchor is anything that gives stability or security, anything that keeps (you) from drifting away, etc. An anchor can be a support or something that gives or provides a support. Faith is an anchor and faith always has an anchor of its own.

Your faith must be anchored on someone or something greater, stronger, heavier, higher, bigger, better, wiser, an omnipotent, that can support, uphold, sustain and/or answer you without intimidation, fear or failure. An anchor cannot fail. A faith-anchor must be ready at all times, omnipotent and available all the times or else it will disappoint you when you need it most. God is the only One that fits these requirements. There is no other. You cannot trust a carved wood, a wrought iron or golden ornament to answer you in day of trouble, sickness and adversity.

Without an anchor-of-faith, your faith might not stand for a long time. It might drift when it faces or encounters the winds of adversity, the powers in the air, land and sea, and all other evil powers and temptations. There are such powers everywhere; whether you believe it or not. There is only One True Anchor that I know of: He is the God of Heaven and earth and there is only one name that has become a true anchor to all that come to Him by faith, that name is **Jesus**. You can trust Him, believe Him, rely on Him, depend and repose on Him. He will secure your faith and bring you stability and a living hope for the future and eternity. He is the Rock of Ages, the Beginning and the End, the First and Last, the Ever Present One, I am that I am, the Maker, Creator, Owner, and Sustainer of the ends of the earth. He is the Author and Encourager of our faith. Hebrew 12:2. He is the Anchor you can trust at all times. He is the anchor you need for your faith to be stable, secure and not wobble or drift in troublous times.

Yes I Can

There are certain words, phrases and sentences that I call faith-words. Faith-words are power-words that motivate and sustain our faith. They are action words. Faith-words have helped me a lot in my own walk of faith. They include positive and negative faith-words; but by far positive faith-words are more desirable and more productive than the negative and destructive words.

POSITIVE FAITH-WORDS   NEGATIVE-FAITH-WORDS

POSITIVE FAITH-WORDS	NEGATIVE-FAITH-WORDS
I can.	I can't.
I will.	I won't.
I am able.	I don't think so.
God is able.	It is not the will of God.
It is possible.	It's impossible
I am forgiven	I don't think God can forgive me.
I forgive you	I can't forgive that.
Nothing is impossible.	It can't be possible.
I will make it.	I can't try that.
This is God's will	Maybe it is not the will of God.
God will do it again.	Prayed before, nothing happened.
I am confident	I am afraid.
I will succeed.	I've tried before and failed.

These and many other phrases like them will either boost your faith or destroy and discourage our faith. The phrases I can or can't are so powerful that much of our successes or failures in life come from them. When you say or think you can't, you immediately and automatically shut off your faith for success in that venture. Even if you try very earnestly with that mindset you may never succeed in that adventure, because you do not believe in yourself or in the ability of your anchor to sustain your faith. . The scripture says "I can do all things through Christ who strengthens me." Philippians 4:13. It is better to die in your faith than to live in your unbelief and doubts.

Word of Faith

The scripture says God created the world by the word of his power. Words are things. Words are powerful. Words are creative. They are very powerful instruments of creativity. Your word is your power and your power is the power of God within you, and is irresistible. There are different kinds of powers:

Word Power
Mind Power
Faith /Spiritual Power
Physical Power
Military Power
Financial Power, etc.

By far the greatest powers are those within you, that is, the mind, faith and word powers and they are readily available within each one of us. Use them to your benefit. With these you can create all other powers as you desire. Words clothe your faith and give it expression in the physical. They convey the unseen power of your faith to the outside world. Therefore, always use words that convey faith. Faith always finds expression in words, affirmations and actions.

Faith and Motivation

Faith is the source of all motivation. When your mind is full of faith your motivation is very high and when your mind is faith deficient, your motivation is usually low. When your faith is low, you become low in self-esteem, and confidence. If your faith is low, you will begin to slip into fear, unbelief, doubt, anxiety and worry. The presence of these negatives will wipe out your faith completely. These negatives do not help your faith in any way so you do not allow them even for a moment.

Faith inspires motivation and motivation drives ambition and ambition pilots achievement and success. Faith properly harnessed will lift you up to higher levels of achievements you had never dreamt of. Faith is a very crucial element of success in everything we do in life.

Your faith is your success wand. Wave it over your thoughts, words and plans and success will follow. All successful people are men and women of faith and confidence. Believe it or not that is a truism. Remember this; you must develop faith in yourself and in God. The battle of life is never won alone. Scripture says, "Two are better than one, because they have a good reward for their labor; for if they fall, one will lift up his companion. But woe to him who is alone when he falls, for he has no one to help him up..." Ecclesiastes 4:9-12. For this reason you must have an anchor to your faith. Faith without an anchor cannot stand for a long time because it is baseless and is an assumption.

The ability to see things in the spirit, or with the inner faith-eye, is called revelation, inspiration, hunch or vision. This ability allows you to focus on deep and infinite realms of the spirit and engage them with your mind and 'conscience.' It is there that visions are molded into reality. The ability to change or effect things in the spirit is called Faith. Everyone has a measure of those gifts. When you combine faith and inspiration you produce what I call "faith-inspiration."

Faith-inspiration is the ability to see a thing in the spirit and capture it in the natural state. This ability comes with dedication, perseverance and inward concentration. As big as these words sound, they are easily mobilized. This is the creative and higher realm of the faith life which all should aspire to live in. Therein is your life actualized.

Faith and 'The Will'

What is 'The Will'?

The 'Will' is described as power of the mind, volition, desire, choice, resolve, wish, command, intention, decision, discretion, prerogative, determination, commitment, etc. It is the power or seat of decision-making and risk taking. Without the will it is difficult to make and stand by your decision.

The 'Will' is an aspect of the mind that controls decisions or decision- making. Decision making or making up your mind goes with definiteness of purpose and resoluteness. A definite decision must have a definite objective or purpose. Faith works always with the Will and the other component of the mind namely: the intellect and the emotion. There can be no faith without the action of the Will. When the mind: Intellect, Will and the Emotions are working together in a perfect state of harmony, faith is activated and every prayer and/or decision receives immediate approval. Faith works best and always with the Will. The Intellect gathers information, the Will takes decision, the Emotion energizes the spirit and faith takes action. This is the mental process toward the release of faith for any operation or project. You have heard it said "Where there is the Will, there is a way" This statement stems from the fact that there is always a possibility once a decision is reached. The Will and faith are integrally connected. The Will and a definite decision are crucial to the operation of faith.

Faith and Decisions

Faith application requires a definite decision. Faith action is always preceded by a definite and decisive decision. If faith action is not definite and decisive the result may be delayed. Indecision is a sign of doubt mindedness, lack of confidence, fear or lack of courage and weak faith or weakness. Any of these is capable of diminishing, derailing and even destroying your faith. Without a definite decision, you cannot take a major step of faith required to actualize your dreams or visions. God told me once, "if you will take a step of faith I will confirm my word' and when I took the action required, I received the breakthrough I was praying for that same day. Before then I was only praying and hoping.

Definite decision is what I call Faith-trigger. Definite decision triggers faith into action. Your life today is as a result of the choices and decisions you made in the past. He cannot become a man or woman of faith who cannot make up his mind promptly and take decisive actions or risks. This statement applies more to me than anyone else reading this book.

Our choices and decisions determine our fate and destiny in life. Indecision is the worst kind of decision because indecision is in itself a decision. Indecision is a decision, not to take a firm stand, on an issue of importance to you because you are waiting on someone else to make the decision or to approve your plans or idea before you embark on the decision. This is where many Christians get it wrong. We wait for God to decide for us. We wait for the pastor to decide our future. We wait for the doctor to decide our health/fate and we wait for the approval of friends before we take a firm stand on what is in our best interest.

While I do not despise the good advice of our pastors, trusted friends and the doctors, we should know that life is shaped by the actions of faith we take and the decisions that precede it. Procrastinations and indecisions can rob us of the power of definite decision and faith. No one can escape taking risks in his life time because risks are normal and integral part of life itself. Risk-taking builds faith and faith demands courage and firm decisions.

Indecision is one of the major causes of failure in life. No one is born to fail but we make daily decisions that will affect our success or failure in life. Prompt and firm decisions are required in majority of the choices we make and the path of life we choose.

Procrastination is putting off to tomorrow what should have been done yesterday. Procrastination like indecision is a decision in itself. It is a decision [but a poor decision] not to commit to a definite decision or make a decision at all. Slow decision making has a reverse effect of prompt and definite decision, firmness of choices and decision.

Decision making goes with resoluteness, determination, courage, strong-mindedness, strength of will and character, emotional stability, firmness of purpose, unwavering commitment, forceful and incisive faith in oneself. Indecision on the other hand has all the evidences of hesitancy, uncertainty, fluctuation of opinions, ambivalence, uncertainty, doubt, shillyshallying and weakness of will and character. It will be very beneficial to us to study our own individual decision making characteristics and make adjustments and changes when and where necessary.

Not long ago I found myself in this dilemma of making a definite decision. We were about to hold a block party and as a leader of the group I was convinced by one of the organizing members Aliya, to bring in a live band [musical instruments]. All the arrangements were concluded and we were ready to go. But at the last minute when everything was set, someone else who was not with us during the planning stages suggested that we play music from CDs instead of live instruments for the convenience of it and other logistical reasons. I quickly agreed, changed my mind, called and cancelled the live band agreement unilaterally. If not that Aliya who proposed the live band stood firm on that decision, the band wouldn't have played in the that event.

Although the inclusion of the CD music played a key role in the festivities as the band was late in arriving, that was a lesson for me on firmness of decisions. Firm decisions pay off at last. Don't be cut in the web of indecisions, procrastinations and weak decisions. Reach your decisions fast, promptly and stick to it.

Faith and Risk Taking

One of the benefits of faith is its ability to inspire risk-taking. Risk is the mother of success and achievement. There is no risk without a higher level of faith-inspiration. Every risk you have taken was preceded by a very high degree of faith energy and higher vibrations of thought. If we can make our lives risk-abound instead of risk-averse, we would produce a much high rate of success in life. Risk-taking should be a given in the lives of those who want to succeed. The challenges we face have a way of boosting our lives if we overcome them by the actions of our faith. Calculated risks should be the norms of human existence.

The opposite is also true. Those who are risk averse tend not to achieve notable things in life. The risk averse is usually timid, fearful and doubtful. No one can succeed in life without taking a good measure of risks in their lifetime. Risk-taking is not a bad thing at all; on the contrary, it is a blessing and the gateway to success, joy and prosperity. I wished I knew what I now know; I would have been operating at a higher level of faith and would have taken much greater risks than I have done so far.

The reason some people fail when they take risk is because of insufficient or inadequate level of faith. When you take a risk that is not sufficiently and adequately backed by full faith, then the results may not be as expected or even lead to outright failure. There is nothing as half faith or what people call 'half-heartedness in the application of faith. Faith must be full or complete or not at all. Faith can be small, faith can be ignorant but it must be full to produce the desired result.

Risk is the super-action or physical equivalent of your faith-action. Risk brings out the man or woman in you, the real you. When you take a risk you subdue the power of fear, doubt and unbelief and rise to a new level of self-discovery, power, confidence and achievement. Risk-taking helps you to learn and discover some secret things about your hidden and untapped potentials. You will discover that you are a diamond in the rough and a miracle waiting to happen. It is in taking risks that you discover who you truly are and the extent of the power you are carrying within you. Risk-taking opens the floodgate of your blessings.

Risk taking is not just for the people out there, it is for you also. Yes, I am talking to you reading this book. How many risky ventures have you undertaken in the past one year? When I talk about risks, I am talking about well calculated risks and not any reckless, thoughtless and ungodly risks. Not all risks will lead to success as we have noted earlier. There is nothing impossible if you can rise to the level of faith required to clinch the desired result. The risk you take must be consistent with rational and godly pursuits.

Risk taking does not mean stupidity and crazy actions. Risk taking means applying your faith in the best possible way and harnessing your hidden potentials and the boundless resources of the Infinite. Risk taking may be what we need to meet and solve the pressing problems confronting humanity. Risk taking is the engine of discovery and inventions. It applies also in spiritual things as well as natural things. Some risky undertaking must be repeated 10,000 times as Thomas Edison found out before the desired results can come. Do not give up or lose hope if you fail in your first attempt. Persevere, because faith requires perseverance and patience to succeed. Remember practice brings perfection.

Faith and Failure

Faith that brings results is narrow minded and does not accept contrary views and suggestions except they are absolutely in line with your faith objective or better. Once faith is locked into position it does not open its doors to external influences and opinions from the outside. It remains locked in until the goal is achieved. Even if the project fails, faith has not failed, it completed its job except that the information it was working with was probably inadequate, flawed or the timing was not right.

When your faith project fails, you did not fail because a man or woman of faith does not fail. You may have a setback or series of setbacks, but you have not failed and actually cannot fail. The reason people think that they are failures when their projects fail is because people equate project failure with personal failure. When your project fails or your prayer was not answered as you hoped, don't give up, rise up and start all over again. Project failure is not personal failure.

There is a difference between project failure and personal failure. A project failure comes as a result of inadequate preparation, insufficient and improper information, inadequate level faith, fear of failure, doubt, inadequate knowledge and a host of other reasons. Personal failure on the other hand is the result of wrong thinking, indecision, poor judgment, insufficient risk-taking, wrong belief system and lack of confidence among others. The scripture says "For as he thinks in his heart, so is he…" Proverbs 23:7.

There is nothing like personal failure. All failures are failures of something; failure to rise up when you fall, failure to try again, failure to take more risks or becoming risk averse, etc. You can fail in a project and still hold your head high. A man that has his bearings right cannot fail. Man is not created to fail. Man is created with a resilient spirit that can rise after a terrible fall. A man has not failed until he dies without achieving his own desire. Even when you declare yourself a failure and the whole world pronounces you a failure, I declare that you are not a failure.

You cannot be considered a failure until your mind is dead because faith never dies. You are not created to fail because you are created to be a creator who never fails. Are you a creator? If you have the faith and ability to change your circumstances and situations, then you cannot fail. The only time I can consider you a true failure is if you are dead and did not create a single thing before you died. Adam and Eve failed because they died spiritually. If they had asked for forgiveness, they would not have become such great failures. You are a failure if you are dead both spiritually and physically.

There is always hope for the living. Ecclesiastes 9:4 says "For to him that is joined to all the living there is hope: for a living dog is better than a dead lion." Also in Jeremiah 17:13 it reads "O LORD, the hope of Israel, all that forsake thee shall be ashamed, and they that depart from me shall be written in the earth, because they have forsaken the LORD, the fountain of living waters."

You are not a failure if you have passed a single exam in your life, if you have children, if you have thought of something and did it, if you still have hope of success in this life, if you have tried something and failed and are still alive, if you have tried any project, no matter how small, and succeeded, if you are still breathing as you read this book, if this book is motivating you and so on. Failure is only a state of the mind. You can change it when you wish, even right now.

The notion of failure is a lie from the pits of hell. It must not hold you any longer in bondage. Free your mind and start thinking and believing in yourself again. Free yourself of the guilt of failure. You are a success. Did I hear you say that? Hmmm let me hear you say it again; I am a success no matter what people say. Now this is faith. When your belief system is wrong then you cannot but be a failure and when your belief system is right then you are a success. It is only a matter of time before you perfect your plans for the manifestation of you success stories. This is not rocket science. It is pure logic. It is faith science. Failure is a mistake to be corrected.

Success is a journey and a story. Achievement is transitory. What means so much to you today, the moment you achieve it, it becomes a story and may not motivate you that much again. Your motivation must only continue to be your faith. No one is too old to start all over again. A man of positive faith will live longer, healthier and happier.

When you try your hands at some project, no matter how passionate you feel about it and it did not succeed, you did not fail, the project failed but you succeeded. This is because you learned how not to do it and it offers your another opportunity to do it again and again until you succeed. Thomas Edison has taught us after 10,000 failures at a single project, that project failure is not the end of that project rather the beginning of its understanding.

He also taught us that project failure is not in any way a personal failure. Even a marriage failure is not a personal failure. Let me restate here that 'No Failure is a Personal Failure.' You are not wired to fail but you can think and believe yourself to failure. You can only fail if you think and believe you have failed. Everyone at some point in life has failed in something, it doesn't matter what; failure is failure. It depends on what you do with your life after a failure. Success and failure are integral parts of life and existence. Some falls are harder than others but you are not meant to remain there and moan.

Faith is the only antidote against failure that is ever known to man. There is no other antidote. Money fails, man fails, education fails, strength fails, wisdom fails, weapons fail, beauty fails, love can fail if it is not applied with faith, hope can fail if it is not applied with faith. Faith sustains or undergirds every other virtues and emotions. That is how important and how powerful faith is to our existence on this planet earth. Faith is the courage, tenacity and resiliency to do things or carry on even after a major disaster. Faith is the courage to continue even after they have given up on you. Your faith will never give up on you because faith believes in you.

CHAPTER 7

FAITH FOR HEALING

Faith-healing is perhaps the most widely known and heard of; and the most misunderstood of all faith applications. Faith healing is very common in the Charismatic Christian circles but repudiated in some Catholic and non-Christian religions. This is sadly because faith healing has been going on since the beginning of days and was popularized by Jesus Christ and the Apostles till date. Yet people choose not to believe and close their minds and withhold their faith from performing its natural functions.

Jesus was and His name is today the master of faith healings. "And his name through faith in his name hath made this man strong, whom ye see and know: yea, the faith which is by Him hath given him this perfect soundness in the presence of you all."Acts:3:16. Jesus told His followers let it be done unto you according to your faith. "And when He had come into the house, the blind men came to Him. And Jesus said to them, "Do you believe that I am able to do this?" They said to Him, "Yes, Lord." Then He touched their eyes, saying, "According to your faith let it be to you." And their eyes were opened. And Jesus sternly warned them, saying, "See that no one knows it." Matthew 9:29. Jesus repeatedly used faith and required faith of all people who came to him for healing.

What Is Faith-Healing?

Faith healing is the supernatural way of receiving healing with or without medication and other physical or natural ways of healing like surgeries, therapy, etc. Faith healing is man's true and natural way of healing. Before the advent of modern medicine and pharmacy, faith healing was in practice. Faith healing is receiving the healing that has already been appropriated by the stripes; bruises, death and resurrection of Jesus Christ now packaged and delivered through His name.

God the father heals, Jesus (faith in His name) heals and faith in the word of God heals. Faith healing is the process of receiving divine healing by believing the word of God and placing your faith rightly on the name of Jesus and putting action to your faith. The action may include prayer, fasting, going to a crusade ground, or any other necessary action. It is not the action that heals. God heals. The name of Jesus heals. Faith in the word of God is what heals your sickness and not necessarily the prayer. Prayer is only an avenue of faith expression.

People spend precious time arguing whether it is faith or God that heals. It is God through faith in the name of Jesus that heals. Our healing has already been perfected and paid for in advance. Our healings have already been paid for and you can only receive it through faith in the name of Jesus. "For it is God who works in you both to will and to do His good pleasure." Philippians 2:13. "Who Himself bore our sins in His own body on the tree, that we, having died to sins, might live for righteousness—by whose stripes you were healed." 1 Peter 2:24.

Faith for healing is one of the most common forms of faith that people know about, yet many people struggle with it. The body is built in such a way that it responds readily to the internal stimuli of faith. Our faith when properly place in God will heal us of practically any disease. This is because our human systems and organs were formed in an atmosphere of faith-engineering. Faith-engineering is the process of manufacturing things without tools and without active participation or intervention of human technology. It is all done automatically by faith. The cells in our body respond readily to the 7th Sense. Cells see, hear, communicate and respond to one another without the help of any eternal/physical instructions or directives. Spirits also communicate with each other that is why one spirit can heal another when they communicate spiritually.

The brain, as small as it is, is the most amazing machine ever built yet without any tools or machines. The power of the 7th Sense has remained basically untapped, unexplored, and grossly under utilized. Had the power of the human faith been studied and developed as the power of the physical body has, there will cease to be hunger, crime, sicknesses and diseases, wars, and the greed for money or at least reduced them to the barest minimum. The reason is that every one will have the natural/spiritual ability to get what he she desires and/or create or cause to come into existence the object of his desire.

There is a tremendous power in divine faith. The power of faith is the power of the future. The power of creative faith is still very much in the distant horizon given man's over dependence on the physical rather than the spiritual, the visible rather than the invisible and on medications rather than on faith-healing etc.

Man is created to function with a double personality i.e. physical and spiritual perceptive abilities but he lost the better part of his spiritual which is actually where his sensory perceptions are more acute and intense. When man is using or operating in his spiritual or 7th Sense, he is sharp sighted, keen sensed, very discerning, shrewd, intuitive, sensitive, astute and ingenious. He is equally stronger, more powerful, more purposeful, and wiser, with higher acumen than when he is not. Those who operate on this level have greater peace and ease of inventions in any vocation of life and not necessarily scientific inventions only. Every vocation has its own geniuses.

The seventh sense is man's natural and normal highest sense. The first five senses are appendages. Most animals which did not lose their inner senses rely more on them than their physical senses, so man's inner senses are much sharper than the physical. In this way the dog can sense things it does not see and the snake can perceive things it cannot hear. So was man or should I say so is man. The 7th Sense provides us with a higher sense-ability.

Has man lost his spiritual capacity and perceptibility completely? Can He still operate in, reclaim or restore some of it? Can man still connect with the divine in some meaningful and intelligent ways? My answer is yes; it is possible, but requires some hard work and sacrifice. In every generation there have always arisen men and women who by accident or design have flirted with the spiritual and have been able to access their 7th Sense and the power and the peace of that realm of existence. My prayer is that God will help us all and open our understanding to the reality and importance of our true nature and the place of the seventh sense in our daily living and in our spiritual relationship with our spiritual Father-God.

Benefits of Faith Healing

It is a fact that faith healing boosts the immune system or functions. Faith healing is the cheapest and most effective form of healing. In many instances the healing is instant, spontaneous and automatic. It does not have side effects. Faith healing is a faith booster and faith multiplier. It is a strong aid to evangelism and church growth. It promotes wellness and optimizes overall wholeness and well-being. It promotes courage and peace of mind and helps recipients to deal more effectively with their malady, fears, doubt, pain and their anxiety. The belief in faith healing creates some sense of optimism and expectation in the believer thereby helping to boost endurance and inner strength. In most cases healing by faith is complete and thorough and without traces of the malaise.

Believing in faith healing is good for your spiritual, physical and emotional wellbeing. Those who have ongoing belief in faith healing attract to themselves divine power, energy and fortitude to live and carry on. Faith healing is very powerful because of the direct intervention of divine energy into our physical body. It promotes peace, joy, comfort, and a sense of worthiness and divine acceptance. It raises hope and increases faith for tomorrow. It creates personal conviction in the existence of the God of all creation. Faith healing removes depression occasioned by the adverse effects of serious or prolonged illness on the mind and emotions.

Faith healing does more good than medicine because it heals the body, the mind and the spirit and puts you in the right frame of mind to succeed in life and business. Faith gives assurance of possibilities, opportunities and outcomes in the name of Jesus. Jesus said, "If you can believe, all things are possible to him that believes." "Therefore I say to you, whatever things you ask when you pray, believe that you receive them, and you will have them." Mark 11:24.

Faith healing can heal any and all types of afflictions including alcoholism, smoking and drug and substance abuse, cancer, AIDS, etc. It can penetrate the deepest parts of our bones and marrow. Every malady is curable through faith. Sometimes faith works in some unusual ways. Some faith healings removes the pains, suffering and worry but leaves the symptoms. I have no explanation for that. I don't know if it is because of lack of complete faith or that the healer chooses to do it that way. Every healing is different and the faith released in each instance is different.

Faith healing helps us cope with adversities and the negative effects of daily living. Faith healing builds self-esteem, emotional strength, maturity, personal stability and resilience. Faith healing helps you to trust God more, makes you confident, and stable; it also makes you humble. Faith healing releases very strong coping mechanisms for any maladjustment, stresses, transition and changes because it builds strong hope for the future.

Absolute faith in God heals and sustains marriages. Couples who together put their trusts in God and faith in their spouses have higher chances of successful and happy marriages. Faith in God, doing and practicing the Word is the recipe for stability, success and happiness in marriage. This assertion means that each partner believes, and practices faith in God personally and together with the other spouse. Success in marriage cannot be left to one partner alone. It cannot be sustainable that way. Faith should be in God and not in the spouse's abilities, income any other or graces. Faith for marriage success requires 100% commitment from each partner, that is, 200% commitment from both partners not 100% as most people assume.

CHAPTER 8

FAITH DEVELOPMENT

To a large extent faith has been seen mainly in terms of spiritual development and spiritual purposes. It has been equated with giving and receiving from God. Of course these are the primary purposes because there is no other way of communicating with God except through faith in His word. As said earlier, faith is the medium of exchange in the spirit world and God being the Father of spirits requires as a prerequisite for approaching and obtaining favor from Him. It is most important and urgently required of us that we pay very close attention on developing our valuable resource for spiritual transactions. Even if you are a professed atheist, you still need faith to do spiritual business.

The scripture says faith comes by hearing the word of God. What you hear determines what kind of faith you will develop. If you constantly hear cursing and swearing words your faith will develop toward the master and king of cursing and swearing –Satan. If you constantly listen to some kinds of rock and hells music, your faith will develop in the god of those music. But if you carefully and consistently hear the word of God and listen to gospel music your faith will also develop in the God of the scripture. For the scripture has said "But without faith it *is* impossible to please Him, for he who comes to God must believe that He is, and that He is a rewarder of those who diligently seek Him." Hebrews 11: 6.

Faith for spiritual development comes from no other source than from the word of God. God inspired His word, God is in His word and God is His word. He watches over His word to perform it. The LORD said to me, "…You have seen correctly, for I am watching to see that my word is fulfilled. Jeremiah 1:12. It is not about the identity of the person using or believing the Word. It is about the Word. For instance God answered and saved the people of Nineveh when they heard and believed the Word of God that was preached by Jonah. While Jonah who knew better and disobeyed the Word found himself in the belly of a great whale. "Now the LORD provided a huge fish to swallow Jonah, and Jonah was in the belly of the fish three days and three nights. From inside the fish Jonah prayed to the LORD his God. He said: "In my distress I called to the LORD and he answered me. From deep in the realm of the dead I called for help, and you listened to my cry." Jonah 1:17, 2:1-2.

Obedience to the Word brings results and builds faith. Every other type of faith is easier to acquire but spiritual faith is more difficult because of what I call 'Distractions of Faith' which we will discuss in a later chapter. Faith for spiritual development comes from hearing and obeying the word of God. Obeying is the action part of faith application. You can hear all you want about the gospel but until you begin to obey and put them to action your pure-faith will not grow much. Acting on or doing the word of God guarantees results.

There can be no spiritual development without faith. Everything we do to develop our spiritual lives actually goes to developing our faith and the ability to hear, receive and obey God. The reason it is so difficult and often requires extended periods of fasting and praying to develop an ounce of higher faith, is because there are faith destroyers and distractions of faith we are contending with. These destroyers and distractors are spirit beings who are or would be affected if we become stronger. They are called demons.

Demons are spirit beings that get bullied, cast out, condemned, chained, and deprived of their host-residences when we get spiritually strong. Our spiritual battles are not with or against flesh and blood. "Finally, my brethren, be strong in the Lord and in the power of His might. Put on the whole armor of God that you may be able to stand against the wiles of the devil. "For we do not wrestle against flesh and blood, but against principalities, against powers, against the rulers of the darkness of this age, against spiritual hosts of wickedness in the heavenly places. There-fore, take up the whole armor of God that you may be able to withstand in the evil day, and having done all, to stand." Ephesians 6:10-12.

This passage of scripture gives a window to peer into the spirit world and see what we are contending with. Without faith you can be easily overrun, defeated and/or seriously weakened. Spiritual battles are as real as the physical battles but are worse in that we do not see the enemy we are dealing with the physical eyes. The reason we are surviving is because the enemy has already been defeated and his armor and backbone broken but he is not dead. You will agree with me that a sighted ten year old boy can keep a blind forty year old very miserable because of the sight advantage. This is a part of the reason we are going through all the troubles we are in today.

It is not the will of God that we should be suffering but as long as the devil and his demons are here with us in this world, there is, and will continue to be this warfare. Did I say that the enemy has been defeated, yes, he has. By who? Jesus Christ! Why didn't He kill Satan, I don't know, perhaps his time has not yet come. How does our faith affect him? When we build up the power of our faith, what do we do with the new power that we have? Of course, cast out the devil and demons in our lives, families, church members and anyone else that we can help. And what does it do to the demons, they lose their homes or abode and become homeless, they are bruise, injured, battered, chained, cast into prison, or cast untimely into the abyss, and many other untold punishments meted out to them.

Therefore, for them to keep their places, in your life and family, (remember they do not have very much ammunitions to fight with), they now depend on using deceptions, lies, anger, lust, immoralities, lust for money, incitement to personality clashes, wars, fears, intimidations, doubts, unbelief, sicknesses/diseases, racism, divorce, joblessness, hatred, murder, disobedience to the law and to parents and so many other non-physical weapons to fight us. Family problems and in-fighting, church problems and church split, un-forgiveness and bitterness are some of the many weapons they incite us to use against ourselves. Remember they hardly touch us but they exploit our short sightedness, blindness and human weaknesses, greed, selfish ego to make us fight and destroy ourselves and one another. The higher demons are overcome by faith, blood of Jesus, and word of God.

There are other weapons in their arsenal, they can actually block our prayer and/or withhold, divert, manipulate, siphon and seize some of our blessings. They can also use their human agents to fight and persecute us physically and spiritually. Because most of us do not see or know much of what happens around us in the spirit realm, we fall and fail easily even after the battle has been won for us by Jesus Christ. As long as Satan is in this world, this may be a constant source of concern for humans. But there is hope in Jesus Christ. Christ is the only hope of the world in the battle against Satan.

How did we lose our spiritual sight and the ability to see in the spirit world? Adam was a spirit-man who saw and communed with God on a daily basis until he sinned. He was equipped with eyes that could see both in the spirits and natural. He had no need of faith. Satan deceived Adam and Eve with the lure to give them more spiritual insight and wisdom to know more than God intended for them. God was not at all pleased with their disobedience and, therefore, cut off His direct Spiritual connection with them. From then on their ability to see clearly in the spirit was destroyed and so we all inherited spiritual blindness.

However, Jesus came and restored us back to God and gave us another or a different kind of spiritual eyes to see God, move and interact in the spirit realms. That new kind of sight is called FAITH or the 7th Sense. Now we can look into the spirit realms through the eyes of faith and take hold of spiritual realities through the hands of faith, etc. We should no longer be as blind as we used to be before Jesus came into our lives; or are you still blind because you refused to believe in Jesus Christ. Faith in Jesus Christ is now our natural means of seeing and knowing spiritual things. I will encourage you to develop your spiritual eyes of faith and do not remain in spiritual darkness any more. Faith will open to you a new realm of possibilities and opportunities you never dreamt of previously. For these reasons I call faith the 7TH Sense. Walking and living by faith will free you from the effects of spiritual blindness. Faith for spiritual development comes by hearing the word of God and doing it.

CHAPTER 9

FAITH DISTRACTIONS

Distractions of faith are those things that make us diminish in faith and can even make us lose our faith in ourselves or in God. Distractions of faith distract us from concentrating on the deep inner things that build up our faith. Some of them include: false religious teachings that deny Jesus as the Son of God. This practice is most dangerous because if you deny the one through whom you will receive spiritual faith, then there is no remedy for your spiritual blindness. Jesus himself said, "Therefore I said to you that you will die in your sins; if you do not believe that I am He, you will die in your sins." John 8:24. The Message.

Other distractions of faith include: wrong thinking such as: doubt, unbelief, fear, worry, anxiety, discouragement, impatience, un-forgiveness, presumption, superstitions, lack of spiritual concentration, absent mindedness, hopelessness, lying, sin or wrong standing with God and self limiting thoughts and beliefs. Distractions of faith weaken our spiritual energy and power of inspiration and motivation.

They make us lose focus. Faith demands concentration, absolute concentration on the object of your need or desire and in the Infinite One.

Strong faith, mountain moving faith, prayer answering faith, requires a good measure of concentrated faith. There can be no powerful manifestation of faith without a deep concentration on the Word and the object of concern and prayer. Faith is the firm foundation upon which everything that makes life worth the while hangs. It is our handle on what we cannot see. Distractions of faith distract our ability to believe, concentrate and have confidence in God's Word and in ourselves. Spiritual faith is anchored on God's Word and never in anything else. For that reason everyone can receive faith and miracles. They are not the exclusive preserve of any special kinds of persons. Faith is based on the Word, written or spoken. You can read it, hear it, speak and do it yourself. It is that easy and simple.

Distractions of faith make us focus on wrong and negative values and on our inadequacies and inabilities, such as, "I can't", "it's not possible", "I failed before", "it's hopeless", "I'm a sinner", "it won't work", etc. Distractions of faith can come from within you, other people and worse of all from Satan and demons. The good news is that "And they overcame him by the blood of the Lamb and by the word of their testimony, and they did not love their lives to the death." Another translation says "They triumphed over him by the blood of the Lamb and by the word of their testimony they did not love their lives so much as to shrink from death." Revelation 12:11 NIV. The result of correct application of faith is always victory. Victory awaits any man or woman of faith. Victory awaits any child of faith. Victory waits any congregation of faith without exception. Distractions of faith accounts for much of the problems believers face. If the devil can distract you, he can defeat you in that area of life. There are no exceptions. Some of the distractions of faith can also be destroyers of faith.

Trials of Faith

Trial of faith is another challenge faith faces. Trial of faith comes when God is testing our faith in Him. This is when God wants to prove our faith or test our resolve to live by faith in Him regardless. In such situations God would ask us to do some impossible or humanly unacceptable things that sometimes are difficult to swallow or that defy the five senses. This is where faith comes into play. For example, consider this vision by Ezekiel the prophet:

"The hand of the LORD was on me, and he brought me out by the Spirit of the LORD and set me in the middle of a valley; it was full of bones. He led me back and forth among them, and I saw a great many bones on the floor of the valley, bones that were very dry. He asked me, "Son of man, can these bones live?" I said, "Sovereign LORD, you alone know." Then he said to me, "Prophesy to these bones and say to them, 'Dry bones, hear the word of the LORD! This is what the Sovereign LORD says to these bones: I will make breath to enter you, and you will come to life. I will attach tendons to you and make flesh come upon you and cover you with skin; I will put breath in you, and you will [live] come to life. Then you will know that I am the LORD.'

So I prophesied as I was commanded. And as I was prophesying, there was a noise, a rattling sound, and the bones came together, bone to bone. I looked, and tendons and flesh appeared on them and skin covered them, but there was no breath in them.

Then he said to me, "Prophesy to the breath; prophesy, son of man, and say to it, 'This is what the Sovereign LORD says: Come, breath, from the four winds and breathe into these slain, that they may live.' So I prophesied as he commanded me, and breath entered them; they came to life and stood up on their feet—a vast army.

Then he said to me: "Son of man, these bones are [believers] the people of Israel. They say, 'Our bones are dried up and our hope is gone; we are cut off.' Therefore prophesy and say to them: 'This is what the Sovereign LORD says: My people, I am going to open your graves and bring you up from them; I will bring you back to the land of Israel. Then you, my people, will know that I am the LORD, when I open your graves and bring you up from them. I will put my Spirit in you and you will live, and I will settle you in your own land. Then you will know that I the LORD have spoken, and I have done it, declares the LORD." Ezekiel 37: 1-14. The story above was an impossible situation that defied the five senses, but shows how sovereign in His ways God can be when he decides to test our faith. There is no limit to what he can ask of us. Or consider the case of Abraham who was asked to sacrifice the only son of his old age to God. The chances of his getting another one were equal to one-in-a-million. Let's read: "Sometime later God tested Abraham. He said to him, "Abraham!" "Here I am," he replied. Then God said, "Take your son, your only son, whom you love—Isaac—and go to the region of Moriah. Sacrifice him there as a burnt offering on a mountain I will show you."

Early the next morning Abraham got up and loaded his donkey. He took with him two of his servants and his son Isaac. When he had cut enough wood for the burnt offering, he set out for the place God had told him about. On the third day Abraham looked up and saw the place in the distance. He said to his servants, "Stay here with the donkey while

I and the boy go over there. We will worship and then we will come back to you."

Abraham took the wood for the burnt offering and placed it on his son Isaac, and he himself carried the fire and the knife. As the two of them went on together, Isaac spoke up and said to his father Abraham, "Father?" "Yes, my son?" Abraham replied. "The fire and wood are here," Isaac said, "but where is the lamb for the burnt offering?" Abraham answered, "God himself will provide the lamb for the burnt offering, my son." And the two of them went on together. When they reached the place God had told him about, Abraham built an altar there and arranged the wood on it. He bound his son Isaac and laid him on the altar, on top of the wood. Then he reached out his hand and took the knife to slay his son. But the angel of the LORD called out to him from heaven, "Abraham! Abraham!" "Here I am," he replied. "Do not lay a hand on the boy," he said. "Do not do anything to him. Now I know that you fear God, because you have not withheld from me your son…" Genesis 22-1-12.

Let us also consider the case of Job who lost everything he had including ten children and all the wealth of the wealthiest man in his day because Job was the wealthiest man in the world of his day according to scripture. But during the period of his trial he lost all and was afflicted with terrible diseases. "And the LORD said to Satan, "Behold, all that he has is in your power; only do not lay a hand on his person." So Satan went out from the presence of the LORD. Now there was a day when his sons and daughters were eating and drinking wine in their oldest brother's house; and a messenger came to Job and said, "The oxen were plowing and the donkeys feeding beside them, when the Sabeans raided them and took them away—indeed they have killed the servants with the edge of the sword; and I alone have escaped to tell you!"

While he was still speaking, another also came and said, "The fire of God fell from heaven and burned up the sheep and the servants, and consumed them; and I alone have escaped to tell you!" While he *was* still speaking, another also came and said, "The Chaldeans formed three bands, raided the camels and took them away, yes, and killed the servants with the edge of the sword; and I alone have escaped to tell you!" While he was still speaking, another also came and said, "Your sons and daughters were eating and drinking wine in their oldest brother's house, and suddenly a great wind came from across the wilderness and struck the four corners of the house, and it fell on the young people, and they are dead; and I alone have escaped to tell you!" Then Job arose, tore his robe, and shaved his head; and he fell to the ground and worshiped. And he said:

"Naked I came from my mother's womb,

And naked shall I return there.
The LORD gave, and the LORD has taken away;
Blessed be the name of the LORD."
In all this, Job did not sin nor charge God with wrong."
Job 1:12-22.

The good thing about God's trials is that He will always stay with you all through the period of the trials. He said in the book of Isaiah "When you pass through the waters, I will be with you;
And through the rivers, they shall not overflow you. When you walk through the fire, you shall not be burned, nor shall the flame scorch you. For I am the LORD your God..."
Isaiah 43:2.

God does test his people from time to time and no one is exempt from this godly training and exercise. The more or the closer we walk with God, the more we are tested and the better we become in His sight. However, trials of faith could ruffle your feathers or ridicule you in the eyes of people who do not understand the trials of faith.

There are many other instances that God tested the faith of His people including: David, Daniel, Shadrach, Meshach, Abednego, Paul, and even Jesus the Christ. The list is endless. Therefore know now that not all afflictions that come to a child of God are as a result of sin but could also be a trial of faith. The question every believer should ask him/herself is: Is this a trial or a distraction? If you can correctly discern the source of what you are going through, you will overcome it at last.

CHAPTER 10

FAITH HINDRANCES

Fear

Fear and doubt are two enemies of faith that are ever present wherever faith operates. Fear is an emotional reaction or apprehension to a situation, news, person, place, and/or object, etc. It is an aversion of some sort that can disarm and weakens the body, mind and spirit and can arouse the feeling of hopelessness, panic, depression and anxiety. Fear is a terrible emotion. The scripture calls it a spirit and warns that it is not from God. "For God has not given us a spirit of fear, but of power and of love and of a sound mind. 2 Timothy 1:7.

Fear Analysis

In my book "The Amazing Power of Grace," I described fear as false evidences appearing as real in these acronyms.

F - False

    E – Evidence(s)

        A – Appearing

            R – Real

To really understand and overcome fear, every one of us must conduct a fear analysis every time we are faced with fear and doubt. Fear is a very destructive influence upon our spirit, mind and body. Fear is the negative counterpart of faith. Because our spirits control our actions, words and faith, we must consciously and intentionally examine our spirit to analyze our fears. The scripture reads "God is our refuge and strength, an ever-present help in trouble. Therefore we will not fear, though the earth gives way and the mountains fall into the heart of the sea, though its waters roar and foam and the mountains quake with their surging." Psalm 46: 1-3.

What Is Fear Analysis?

To analyze means to beak up or separate things (whole things) into parts or pieces and examine the parts intensely to find out their make or make up, nature, functions, interrelationships, etc. It is to break down, dissect, study, investigate, evaluate and interpret the results or findings in order to make informed decisions.

The same is true of fear analysis. If you do not understand the thing(s) that make you afraid: its source, strength, composition, duration; you cannot tackle it properly. Every fear has a source and duration. Fear like faith expires unless it is sustained by doubts, anxiety, unbelief and negative spiritual forces. Analysis of your fear gives you a good grip on what you are contending with and helps you to make informed decision as to how you can deal with it, what to do to rid yourself of the burden of the fear and/or what to do to completely destroy and obliterate the source.

When you do a fear analysis you will discover that most of the time, what you are afraid of, is never truly real and in some instances non existent. They are just the imaginations of your heart and the superstitions of your own mind. Many times our minds play up scenarios of what could happen if some (unverified) facts applied. Most fears are not real. They are imaginations of what we think could result if certain conditions would happen or is happening. The truth is that most of them do not and would never happen; and when they do happen, our negative faith or state of mind during those periods helped to bring them to reality.

Remember, fear is a natural emotion just like faith. In fact fear is the opposite of faith. When two or more emotions of the same kind mix or collide in an atmosphere of positive or negative vibration, the energy that is release is always so powerful that they can move mountains for good or for evil. Fear works almost exactly as faith but in the negative and destructive direction. Faith works constructively but fear is destructive.

Whatever you do not believe completely will always cast a shadow of doubt in your mind and foment indecision, anxiety and ultimately fear. In the same vein, whatever you completely believe will clear your mind of indecisions, doubts, anxiety, and fear and ultimately will produce faith. Faith is the absence of indecision, anxiety and fear. Faith is a stress buster. Are you stressed up? Go and do a work of faith.

The reason I advocate for and teacher faith is because we can save ourselves from all kinds of illnesses that are stress induced due to the negative energies released into our bodily functions: mental, emotional and spiritual wellbeing that could cause harm and ill-health. Faith is the energy of life, the true energy of life. Man at birth or creation does not start out with fear. Man starts out as a faith-being until he begins to sin. Then fear comes in. Sin brings the condition of fear.

Every little child believes every thing as he is told until he begins to reason, think and imagine. Adam and Eve did not fear the presence of God in the garden until they began to think, imagine and reason with the devil. Fear is the result of negative thinking and imagination of the negative consequences of our actions, reactions or inactions. Faith on the other hand is the positive thinking and imagination of the positive or righteous consequences and rewards of our action and words.

Fear is the reason for most of the stresses we bear or experience. Wherever and whenever fear is present it will over burden the heart, diminish abilities and capacities to function, create delusions-grandeur, inhibit and/ or accentuates some normal operations of our bodily functions. It removes peace, joy and contentment which are key ingredient for mental and spiritual stability and operations.

On the other hand, faith maintains or restores peace of mind, emotional stability, contentment, self confidence and spiritual wellbeing. It empowers love, joy and sound mind which are the fundamentals to a healthy living and effective functioning of the mind, spirit and body. For these reasons faith-healing is so effective because it restore the whole being to its original or normal state and develops hope, stabilizes wobbling faith and increases self worth and self confidence. Because fear has the opposite capacity as faith, it should never be accepted or accommodated. However, fear will always be with people who accept it because it works subtly in the subconscious through what we see, hear, and/or imagine. You have the right and power to reject it the moment you sense it.

Faith comes by hearing the Word of God but fear comes by hearing, seeing, thinking and imagining negative things from any source. The word imagination came from the root word imagine or image. When you are engaged in the process of imagination, your mind concocts and fabricates ideas and scenarios of possibilities that could happen if certain parameters come together and that leaves you with the choice of making a decision. The human nature most times fears to dwell on decisions that they cannot handle if the result will be adverse when it happens. The consequences are doubt, anxiety disbelief and eventually fear. When these factors are present there will follow a correspondent negative action or reaction to the negative things we have imagined. Faith in God can remove our fears to the barest minimum. The scriptures say "What, then, shall we say in response to these things? If God is for us, who can be against us? Romans 8:31. "In God have I put my trust: I will not be afraid what man can do unto me" Psalms 56:11.

The mind is a terrific machine or engine. It can manufacture, formulate, fabricate, scheme, design, blend, fashion and dream up anything. It has the ability to harness and acquire information from both the natural and the invisible and brew scenes and scenarios of impossible proportions. It is therefore, our responsibility to research and analyze the sources and consequences of our fears. As mentioned earlier, most of them are false evidences that appear as real.

Fear has power, intensity and torment. I wrote in my book 'the Amazing power of Grace' "What is your source of fear? What is your reason of being afraid? Have you ever taken the time to find out what you are really afraid of? Have you taken the time to find out why you are afraid of this thing or that person? When did the fear start and how did it begin? Can you face it when you find out? If you cannot face it, you will never be able to overcome it. If you cannot face it, do you need help? Can you find adequate help to deal with it once and for all? These are very pertinent questions you have to answer before you can rid yourself of debilitating fears.

Fear is a spirit that lives and works within your conscience and emotions. It can paralyze the intellect, destroy the will, cancel ambition, disgrace a man and stifle emotions. Fear can also supplant reason, cause suspicion, anger and frustration. It has ruined marriages, destroyed trust, separated friends and family, failed pupils in exams and denied people of joy, peace, love and friendship. Fear can make a man impotent and a woman sterile. Fear brings false accusations and can cause you to tell lies. In fact, every lie is the result of fear of something, someone, punishment, or other reasons."

I believe that some of the diseases that cannot be detected under the microscope are in part due to fears whether real or imagined. These fears hide within our emotions and within our needs, desires, and aspirations and torment us. It's time to stand up to them and get rid of them. There are only two things that can happen when you face up to your fears. They will either destroy you or you destroy them. They will ruin you any way if you don't destroy them. Sin can cast such dangerous fears upon our souls and could cause untold stress to our systems and organs.

However, fear can be mastered, controlled and destroyed. Do not allow your fear to master and destroy you, but destroy your fears with your faith. It is that serious. The faith that destroys fear stems from the fact that you know, that you know that God is ever present with you. God is on your side. God is for you and He cares about you. God is mindful of you. The Psalmist said "When I consider Your heavens, the work of Your fingers, the moon and the stars, which You have made, what is man that You are mindful of him, and the son of man that You visit him? For You have made him a little lower than the angels, And You have crowned him with glory and honor. You have made him to have dominion over the works of Your hands. You have put all things under his feet." Psalms 8:3-6. To have faith you must address your fears. God is the source of all faith. God forgives those who come to Him for help.

Fear of Stepping Out

Fear of stepping out is among the worst hindrances to the exercise of faith. If you do not step out of your shell, fear or comfort zone and begin to act on your convictions and faith, you will never see many mighty miracles or the fulfillment of your dreams. Miracles are the bread of God's children. "He replied, "It is not right to take the children's bread and toss it to the dogs." Matthew 15:26. If you believe yourself to be a child of God, you are entitled to receive the God-kind of faith or godly faith. You have the ability to perform and receive miracles by the exercise of your God given faith.

Godly faith is natural to every believer who dares to step out and exercise his/her faith. If you believe the Word of God then you already and potentially possess all the faith you need at least to start practicing your faith life. It is your right of son-ship in the family of God.

Even though we have dealt with fear in a previous chapter, It bears repeating here that fear will rob you of the joy and fulfillment of being a believer. Fear can paralyze your faith and make you impotent to receive healings, blessings, answer to prayers and miracles in the face of God's superabundance.

Faith transcends cultures, languages, races, skin colors and people groups. Wherever faith is found God will be present there and miracles are possible to happen. "Then Peter opened his mouth and said: "In truth I perceive that God shows no partiality. But in every nation whoever fears Him and works righteousness is accepted by Him." In Acts of the Apostles chapter 10 it details how God accepted the gentiles (non Jews) the same way he accepted the Jews. Act 10:34-35.

We have seen people of all races, creeds, cultures, languages and beliefs receive and come to Christ in crusades after crusades and in Churches throughout the world. We have seen Muslims, Jews, Hindus, Sikhs, atheists, witch doctors, African traditionalists; unbelievers who had never heard the name of Jesus give their lives to Christ at the first hearing of the gospel of faith. And we have seen them also receive miracles there and then. Faith and not religion is what God is looking for in His children. Regardless of where we come from, we are all God's children by creation until we rebelled. Many Christians could be in rebellion in refusing to use or exercise their faith adequately. You can be sure of one thing, God is looking for sons and daughters who will believe and act on his Word and be blessed and also become instruments of blessing and service to others.

Standing Your Ground

Standing your ground means standing up to the menacing challenges of doubt and fear. It means believing and keep-believing what the Word of God says concerning your situation, desires and/or prayer and in spite of the boisterous and intimidating situations around you. Regardless of the fact that your doctor has told you that you have six months to live; regardless of the fact that you have no job or just lost your job and the landlord or the bank is threatening. Regardless of the fact that your spouse has been diagnosed with cancer; regardless of whatever scenario you find yourself in, the word of God is always the same and true to itself.

God cannot deny His Word. "He is the Maker of heaven and earth, the sea, and everything in them— he remains faithful forever." Psalm 146:6. "If we are faithless [do not believe and are untrue to Him], He remains true (faithful to His Word and His righteous character), for He cannot deny Himself. 2Timothy2:13. Amplified Bible.

Standing your ground means rejecting and refusing to give up hope like Abraham "Who against hope believed in hope, that he might become the father of many nations, according to that which was spoken, So shall thy seed be. And being not weak in faith, he considered not his own body now dead, when he was about an hundred years old, neither yet the deadness of Sarah's womb: He staggered not at the promise of God through unbelief; but was strong in faith, giving glory to God; And being fully persuaded that, what he had promised, he was able also to perform. And therefore it was imputed to him for righteousness." Romans 4:17-22

Standing your ground means refusing to listen to contrary view when you know that you are standing on the Word because the Word of God must vindicate itself, must defend itself, it's its own interpreter and it will justify your faith in the end. The scripture said, "As it is written, "I have made you a father of many nations" in the presence of Him whom he, Abraham, believed—God, who gives life to the dead and calls those things which do not exist as though they did. Romans 4:17. NIV.

Standing your ground means having a stubborn faith. Faith that does not give up very easily; faith that does not easily forget the goodness of God to us in the past. "That they might set their hope in God, and not forget the works of God, but keep his commandments. And might not be as their fathers, a stubborn and rebellious generation; a generation that set not their heart aright, and whose spirit was not steadfast with God" Psalms 78:7. KJV.

Standing your ground means having a faith that does not limit or down play the power of God. As it is written "… they turned back and tempted God, and limited the Holy One of Israel. They remembered not his hand, nor the day when he delivered them from the enemy. Psalms 78:41-42. KJV. It means not turning your back on him when things are going well with you only to resurface when you need help from Him.

Stand your ground means after you have tried and done everything you possibly can and the results you are seeing are not what you are expecting, stand and wait. The scripture says having done all, stand. "Wherefore take unto you the whole armor of God that ye may be able to withstand in the evil day, and having done all, to stand. Ephesians 6: 13. KJV. When you are standing, your are praying both in the spirit and with knowledge, you are studying the Word, you are praising Him as though you have already received your healing or the job, the house, the child or whatever you are waiting on Him for. Remember Jesus said in Mark 11:24 says "all thing whatsoever you desire when you pray believe that you have received it and it shall be yours".

Standing your ground is waiting for the opportune time and doing all that is necessary and incidental on your part; that is faith. Faith time is test time. When you are exercising faith you are testing and being tested. You are putting the Word of God to the test and God is also putting you to the test at the same time. You want to see the power of God's Word and God wants to see the quality of your resolve to trust and depend on Him even without seeing Him or what you have desired. Remember it is no longer faith if you already see or know the answer to what you are waiting for. It is faith only when you do not see or know where, when, how, and from whom God will do it and you still trust and believe that it shall come even as you have prayed. Standing your ground is very imperative in the exercise of faith.

Anxiety and Nervousness

Anxiety is an unnecessary concern about something of which you do not have control over. It is an apprehension that robs the mind of the ability to function productively and at full capacity. Anxiety is a distress of the soul, a distraction. It makes the body nervous and panicky, fretful and impatient, and destabilizes the whole mental systems.

Being anxious, to a large extent, does not produce any good fruit. Even when people are anxious for a good reason, they have been known to make mistakes over things they can control, just because they were so anxious to get it over with. Good students have been known to fail exams, just because they were so anxious during the exam, they became careless and made many simple mistakes. Anxiety does not serve any faith purposes. It should be avoided at all cost. I presume that I have failed many job interviews because of anxiety. Anxiety works well with worry, and together, they evidence lack of self-control, which in turn is the evidence of lack of faith. Being anxious does not make any situation better; rather, it worsens an already bad situation. When anxiety matures, it turns into worry, and worry is the seed of some emotional ill-health, sleeplessness and failures.

Ego

Ego means self; self importance, self-conceit. From ego comes other nouns e.g. egoism, egotism, egoistic, etc., all of which mean, pride, self- loving, self-obsessed, selfishness, self-centeredness, self aggrandizement, self-serving, self-seeking, arrogance, over-reaching self-esteem, self glorification, superiority complex, boasting, bragging, and much more.

While we encourage positive self-esteem through faith, we discourage egotism in the name of faith. Faith is pure, bold, confident, unassuming, not boastful and not proud. Faith is humble before God and man but strong and assertive when facing evil, trials, turbulence of life, and wicked spiritual powers. The reason faith is humble is because it recognizes that it is a gift from God. You cannot manufacture faith, it comes from God and therefore under the control of the Holy Spirit. Ego or egotism is the opposite of humility. If not checked in time can become pride, a thing that God hates and resists.

Faith works with humility but ego works with pride. In your pursuit of faith, you do not want to pit yourself against the wrath of God because God hates pride but shows favor and grace to the humble. "...God resists the proud, but gives grace to the humble." 1Peter 5:5.

Ego will also deny you the favor of man because people dislike egoistic and proud people. Pride means drawing undue attention to yourself and the gifts that you have received from God and not giving the glory that is due Him. There is a fine line between faith and ego. The main difference between the two is that ego is selfish and carnal while faith is spiritual and honors God. We should be careful of the differences.

Faith works with humility and not pride. False humility is even worse than pride because we may be adding a lie to our pride. We cannot impress God by our high looks or show-off of anything you are or have. God loves humble people. God answers the prayer of humble people. [Read Luke 18:9-14]. God resists the proud and their prayers. 1Peter

5:6 ..."God resists the proud, but gives grace to the humble." Therefore humble yourselves under the mighty hand of God, that He may exalt you in due time, casting all your care upon Him, for He cares for you.

Faith and Unbelief

Unbelief is another hindrance to faith. It means there is no room at all for God or the idea being proposed. Unbelief slams the door at an idea and until that door is opened from the inside, no amount of external pressure can open it. This is because a spiritual door has been shut and that is the reason some marriage problems are difficult to resolve. When the door of forgiveness and reconciliation are shut no man can open it from outside; even God will not force it open. It can only be opened from the inside and by the person who shut it, with the help of the Holy Spirit.

Faith can not work with unbelief because they are not at all compatible. They are diametrically opposed to each other. Unbelief is a complete rejection of an idea in its entirety. You may be wasting your time to try and convince the person at that particular moment, but you can sow a seed of faith whether in word or action that God can use to break the seal on the door of the heart. The devil can lock people's heart and make it difficult to open for a new or a different branch of the same idea.

Faith and Ignorance

There is nothing like an ignorant faith or faith without knowledge. You do not need education to exercise faith. Listen to what the scripture says: But what does it (scripture) say? "The word is near you; it is in your mouth and in your heart, that is, the message concerning faith that we proclaim: If you declare with your mouth, Jesus is Lord, and believe in your heart that God raised him from the dead, you will be saved. For it is with your heart that you believe and are justified, and it is with your mouth that you profess your faith and are saved. As Scripture says, anyone who believes in him will never be put to shame. For there is no difference between Jew and Gentile—the same Lord is Lord of all and richly blesses all who call on him, for, everyone who calls on the name of the Lord will be saved. How, then, can they call on the one they have not believed in? And how can they believe in the one of whom they have not heard? And how can they hear without someone preaching to them?" Romans 10: 8-14.

Faith comes through hearing the gospel and hearing brings knowledge of the truth. Faith is established through believing the truth you hear and know. Finally faith is activated through acting or obeying the truth that you believe. Remember our faith is vertical and to God and not horizontal toward people or things.

Ignorance of The Word of God is one of the main reasons that we do not always have the faith to claim what are rightfully ours and the reason we pray amiss. When I talk about ignorance, I talk about not having sufficient knowledge of God through His Word. You can be very educated and have multiple degrees and even go to church very regularly and still be ignorant of the Word and the things of the spirit.

You may be very active in the church as an usher, leader, administrator, Bible teacher, prayer warrior, etc., and still be spiritually ignorant like a child. These titles do not confer faith. They are just titles for administrative purposes. What confers faith is knowing, believing, acting, and using the Word in any and every circumstance that confronts you. Do not just rely on the messages preached in the church, study the Bible [the Word] and know it. Some preachers don't believe all that they preach. Some people read the Bible like a novel. That is wrong if you want to build a strong faith; even if you cannot quote it verbatim, know it intimately. The scripture says "Study to show yourself competent to God." 2Timothy2:13. There is no excuse for not studying the Word; I do not mean reading the Word.

CHAPTER 11

FAITH BUILDERS

Builders of faith are those activities and persons that help you build your faith. They include: constant study and listening to the Word of God, active prayer life, doing the Word and seeing results, speaking in other tongues, sharing your faith with others, overcoming temptations and fasting. Others are: reading good books on faith, acting on your convictions, having a right standing with God, and a host of other activities that grow faith. Faith comes, faith grows, faith expires, and faith diminishes if not sustained by the above measures.

Builders of faith will grow your faith. As powerful as faith is, it can be fragile. It needs to be nurtured and sustained. There is always room for spiritual growth and development. When faith is stagnant or diminishing, it could have adverse consequences or repercussions. The devil seizes up on the attendant weakness of the individual when faith diminishes and brings afflictions, costly mistakes, doubts and fear; some of which can become destroyers of faith.

Faith Projects

Faith to achieve is the faith expressly released or harnessed toward a particular goal, objective or project. Actually, every faith objective or undertaking is called a PROJECT. What is a Project? A project is a specific task, a proposal, a planned course of action, an organized undertaking. Faith is more effective when it is taken up and executed as projects or in project phases.

A faith-project is the complete dedication of one's absolute, unconditional and complete spiritual energy, mental resources and physical activities towards the attainment of the desired goal. When faith is activated and concentrated in/on one particular and specific goal or project, the result is usually successful and prayers are always answered faster. That has been my own personal experience. This is because faith that is directed and pinpointed acts like a laser beam and can crack any spiritual codes. It has the ability to attract to itself persons or groups, resources and funds, other spiritual forces and ideas to accomplish its objective. It can change people's mind, influence decision making both yours and others and can perform miraculous wonders.

Faith to achieve is the faith to succeed. There is no success without faith input. As said earlier faith is the foundation and power behind all successes. Even those who oppose faith use faith without knowing. Everyone who has succeeded in anything at all in this life had applied faith in some form and in something. When you believe that you can do or try something (a project) whether spiritual or physical, you energize all your faculties and every cell of your body, thereby activating divine resources and intervention to create or bring into manifestation what you desired or believed. Every successful venture is energized by faith.

Faith for success must be sustained until success is achieved. Faith sources its own resources in the course of attaining its objective and could take a while if the resources are far-fetched. Therefore, the scripture says there is need for patience. "For ye have need of patience, that, after ye have done the will of God, ye might receive the promise." Hebrews 10:38:36. Faith works well with patience. You cannot say I have faith and not patience. Both of them work hand-in-hand. Patience is the sustaining power of faith when faith is working behind the scene to realize the desired goal or need, answer our prayer or provide wisdom required to solve the problem.

Faith to Receive Answers to Prayers

Faith that works is the faith that is put to work. If you do not put your faith to work, you will inadvertently put your fears or doubts to work and faith will not work for you. You cannot put the cart before the horse and expect the horse to run. The cart must always be behind the horse and then the horse can run.

When you put your fears, doubts, superstitions and presumptions before your faith in the name of excuses, doubt and procrastination, your faith will not deliver the results you expect. You must always put your fears and excuses behind you and your faith before you and let your faith [I can, I am able, God can do it, God is able, I am healed in the name of Jesus, I'm not giving up, etc.] run.

Faith that works is the faith that gets you excited about the project of your prayer or desire. Here is how you will know that your faith will work for you. Every prayer or project you sincerely believe in, are passionate about, enthusiastic or seriously committed to, and painstakingly pursue will surely bring you the desired result under normal circumstances. Abnormal circumstances require abnormal or mountain moving faith.

Faith is not passive, gloomy, despondent, angry, negative, insincere, shy/ashamed, regretful, and impatient. Faith is positive, energetic, active, passionate, strong and peaceful. Scriptures says, "Proclaim this among the nations: "Prepare for war! Let the weak say, 'I *am* strong." Joel 3:10. And by extension or extrapolation, let the sick say I am healed and the poor, I am rich. Let the old say I am young/strong and the barren, I am a mother. Once said cling to your faith until something happens.

Faith is a clean, positive, action-packed, favor-filled, grace-anointed, power-full and sweet energy. You cannot be applying faith and be crying, frowning, cursing, doubting and fearful at the same time. Faith is a gift of purpose. It is either faith or no-faith. Faith is not hope but hope works with faith. Hope is futuristic while faith is now. Faith works on the instant and expires; hope continues as long as it takes to find adequate faith.

Faith expires after it is applied or put to use but hope continues until faith kicks in and takes over. Hope sustains and supports a desire, idea, wish or project until faith completes its work and the result becomes evident. Faith and hope are two sides of the same coin. They work together and can also work independently. The good thing about faith is that it grows. Even though the work of faith is done very quickly, it continues to add up, it continues to grow in huge incremental. Hope on the other hand, does not grow. Hope continues to remain the same until you consciously decide to give up on the desire, idea, prayer or project.

The faith you use for one project or prayer may not be used for another. You must come up with a fresh faith each time you want to start a new project. When faith is used for a particular project, it expires into your faith-bank and blends with the faith already in the bank so you cannot again use that particular faith but it combines to increase your total reservoir of faith in your faith bank. For this reason faith works in project-like dispensations. That is also the reason why you cannot coast along in prayer. Every prayer must be fresh, intentional and now. Prayer must be accompanied by active faith and persistence. The reason many of our prayers are not answered as quickly as we would want them to is partly because after the initial faith that started the prayer, we relapse into what I call Faith-coasting. Faith-coasting is the belief that the initial faith is still carrying on or may carry you through. In some cases it does but in most others it does not. For this reason you/we must be intentional in every prayer. When we see every prayer and every undertaken or venture as a project, prayer changes from being a chore to being pleasurable engagement. The ramifications of faith are many and varied.

Prayer Projects

Prayer-projects have more chances of quicker answers and success than generic or laundry-list and grocery-list prayers. A grocery-list prayer is something like God bless me, God bless my father, God bless my mother, God bless my sisters, God bless my brothers, God bless my family, God bless our church, God bless my country, God bless the whole world. Obviously this is a good prayer but it lacks definiteness and it is not targeted.

A targeted prayer is definite and direct. Most prayers whether by Christians or not are generic and they lack faith and a definite purpose. They are prayers that plead with God rather than ask. The scripture says "Ask, and it shall be given to you; seek, and you shall find; knock, and it shall be opened to you. For everyone who asks receives, and he who seeks finds, and to him who knocks it shall be opened. Or what man is there among you who, if his son asks for bread, will give him a stone? Or if he asks for a fish, will he give him a serpent? If you then, being evil, know how to give good gifts to your children, how much more will your Father who is in heaven give good things to those who ask Him!" Luke 11:9-13.

Another version puts it this way, "Don't bargain with God. Be direct. Ask for what you need. This isn't a cat-and-mouse, hide-and-seek game we're in. If your child asks for bread, do you trick him with sawdust? If he asks for fish, do you scare him with a live snake on his plate? As bad as you are, you wouldn't think of such a thing. You're at least decent to your own children. So don't you think the God who conceived you in love will be even better? Matthew 7:7-11. The Message.

The problem with generic prayers is that sometimes we are not even interested in some of the people and some of the things we pray for. However, here is a test for a generic prayer. Any prayer that puts you to sleep, no matter the hour of the night is a generic prayer. It does not matter how tired you are.

On the other hand when you embark on a targeted prayer, a project prayer, a prayer of faith, if the need that prompted the prayer is important, very important, very, very important to you, you cannot sleep, in fact sleep will disappear from you. You will be asking it to come and it will be waving you bye. If it is very important, it will wake you up in the middle of the night. Prayer projects come as or with a burden in your spirit; that in turn, motivates and harnesses the desired faith, abilities and supernatural energies that is required to carry it to success.

When I pray God bless my family, who in the family do I want God to bless? Is it you or the spouse you don't really care about or the delinquent child that makes you angry and you will want out of the home as soon as possible or is it yourself who you no longer have as much faith in because of the many failures and sins that trailed your past? With this type of prayer, the power, enthusiasm and faith you require are grossly depreciated and, therefore, would not pass the test of a solid faith prayer. However, if you take these people as a special and different prayer points or projects and at different times, the result would be different.

If you take each person as a prayer project and give him or her a dedicated and undivided prayer attention, and pray until you believe and know that something has or will happen, then you will see and experience the joy of answered prayer. A prayer project like any other project has greater chances of success because you will plan, organize, direct, control and dedicate your faith-time and expectations to receiving the answer. You will set the time within which the result is expected. And if it is not answered immediately, you would have learnt some lessons out of the experience. Prayer projects bring us closer to God than generic prayers.

Take another instance when you pray a prayer like this "God let my enemies die." If God were to answer this prayer, and one of the enemies hindering your progress is your own very self, do you think you will get a quick answer if God does not want to take you at that time? I might add that some might have died as a result of such prayers.

When you make every prayer a project, you will at least do a mental planning of your prayer. You will be intentional and pray with purpose and understanding (except if you are speaking in tongues). You will confess yours or their sins, mistakes and inadequacies as you pray. Then the prayer will be effective because it is targeted and definite. Most of us pray ignorant prayers. God is wise and not foolish as we sometimes are. However, you can get what you ask for if your prayer meets the faith requirements; as small as a grain of mustard seed.

Faith That Works

Faith that receives answers to prayers is faith that works. All prayers receive an answer at the time of prayer. Answers could range from a yes, no, wait patiently, try harder or come higher [importunity]. God says "You shall seek me and find me when you shall search for me with all your heart." Jeremiah 29:13. Giving answers to prayer is God's prerogative. Only God knows when, where, why, how, and what prayer He wants to answer because even Jesus prayed to be relieved from going to the cross and that prayer was turned down. However, Jesus accepted the verdict willingly. God would answer all prayer that come with adequate faith level.

Faith that works is the faith that is based on the Living Word of God. Every other faith could be a probability. It is based on assumptions and probabilities. The Word of God is forever settled in heaven. It is as sure as God Himself. "Forever, O Lord, thy word is settled in heaven." Psalm 119:89. The Word of God is a Guarantee and a guarantor. The reason the Word of God is so authentic is because of the faithfulness of God. God is faithful, very faithful, and extraordinarily very faithful and He guards His Word with His integrity and faithfulness.

God is absolutely dependable and so is His Word. The faithfulness of God's word is not dependent on who you are, what you are, where you came from, the color of your skin, the name of your parents, the degrees and other titles attached to your name. God is more than any of those things that hold sway with mankind. God is God. God is a Spirit. God is not a man. He is above the classes of this world and is in a world of his own in the heavens. You either receive Him or reject Him and in the final analysis He will be there to judge you and none of those things that puffed you up would be there to save you; they would have ceased to exist. But God in His Word lives forever.

God created the world by the power of His Word and has suspended it in the space with all other planets of his making, and governs them as he desires. You can choose to believe or leave it. It does not change anything with Him. The Word says even if we are faithless or refuse to believe He is and will continue to be faithful. "If we are faithless [do not believe and are untrue to Him], He remains true (faithful to His Word and His righteous character), for He cannot deny Himself." 2Timothy 2:13. Even if you choose not to worship Him and He is very thirsty of worshippers, Jesus said that God is able to make stones rise up and worship Him. "And some of the Pharisees called to Him from the crowd, "Teacher, rebuke your disciples." But He answered and said to them, "I tell you that if these should keep silent, the stones would immediately cry out." Luke 19:40. "…For I say to you that God is able to raise up children to Abraham from these stones." Matthew 3:9.

Think of it, there are already billions of angels and humans who now worship Him. Do you think that the absence of your lone praise will make a difference to Him that he should care? But God cares for you not because of you; He cares because He is faithful to Himself and to his Word. God said in Isaiah "I, even I, am He who blots out your transgressions for My own sake; And I will not remember your sins. Put Me in remembrance; Let us contend together; state your case, that you may be acquitted"

Another translation puts it this way, "I, even I, am He Who blots out and cancels your transgressions, for My own sake, and I will not remember your sins. Put Me in remembrance [remind Me of your merits]; let us plead and argue together. Set forth your case, that you may be justified (proved right)." Isaiah 43:25-26. Faith that works must be based on the faithfulness of God's Word to answer your prayers only as He pleases.

The Word works; The Word of God works wonders believe it or not it works. It has worked since the beginning of the time, it has worked for the children of Israel, it worked in Jesus time, it worked for the early disciples and apostles, it is still working now because it is working for me. Because I am a believer I believe the Word will work for you too. Put your faith in it and try it. God is very much active in His business of answering prayers. No one does it better or comes close. Your case is not different, or more difficult; neither has His hand of mercy shortened that He cannot reach you. Listen to what the Word of God says:

"To whom then will you liken Me,
Or to whom shall I be equal?" says the Holy One.
Lift up your eyes on high,
And see who has created these *things,*
Who brings out their host by number;
He calls them all by name,

By the greatness of His might
And the strength of *His* power;
Not one is missing.

Why do you say, O Jacob,
And speak, O Israel:
"My way is hidden from the LORD,
And my just claim is passed over by my God"?
Have you not known?
Have you not heard?
The everlasting God, the LORD,
The Creator of the ends of the earth,
Neither faints nor is weary.
His understanding is unsearchable.
He gives power to the weak,
And to those who have no might He increases strength.
Even the youths shall faint and be weary,
And the young men shall utterly fall,
But those who wait (Hope) on the LORD
Shall renew their strength;
They shall mount up with wings like eagles,
They shall run and not be weary,
They shall walk and not faint. Isaiah 40:25-31.

Faith and Patience

Patience is a staunch ally of faith. Faith sometimes takes time to accomplish its work. For this reason we think that God is slow. However, the scriptures say that God is not slow. "The Lord isn't really being slow about his promise, as some people think. No, he is being patient for your sake. He does not want anyone to (perish) be destroyed, but wants everyone to repent." 2Peter 3:9. New Living Translation. God is never slow. He does things according to His own timing. He is not bound by time and space. Besides God knows the best time to release the answer you are seeking for, in your best benefit and for His glory. We must wait patiently for His timing. If you have done your part well and maintained a solid faith in God and still He did not answer you, it might probably mean He has other plans for you which He will communicate to you in some ways if you are listening.

The Lord our God is the God of faith and patience. Therefore, any one who walks with God and expects to receive from God must in addition to all other virtues imbibe the culture or habit of patience. God cannot be pressured into doing things when it is not his time. Patience is a great virtue. The scripture says "And beside this, giving all diligence, add to your faith virtue; and to virtue knowledge; and to knowledge temperance; and to temperance patience; and to patience godliness…" 2 Peter 1: 5-8.

The virtues of faith and patience are what distinguish between mature and immature believers. An immature believer gives up the moment their own human timing is not met by God but a mature believer continues to keep faith with God until He answers with a yes, no, or wait and be patient. God communicates with us just as any parent would but only through His Spirit. If we are not patient and listening, it is easy to miss Him. Some times He speaks in quietness and in a still small voice.

Patience is not idling away. Patience is waiting actively in prayer and supplication, working toward the desired goal until the results come.

Let me tell you a story of what happened to me when I was preparing to immigrate to Canada. At the time I applied to come to Canada as a Permanent Resident, applications from my country of origin only took about 12 months for processing. However, after few months of my application came the 9/11 incident in the USA, whether related or not, Canada stopped processing applications and began reviewing its immigration laws and policies more stringently for about two or 3 years. By the time they resumed the processing again it was almost three years and by the time I got my visa it was close to five years.

All this time even though hope had faded significantly and the funds saved up for the transition spent, I still held on to my faith that I would still immigrate to Canada. When eventually the letter for reapplication came, I processed it with such speed and assurance because I believed that was God's own time. Some of those who applied together with me initially gave up hope. Some thought the whole program was a scheme. Finally it took about five years to achieve my permanent resident immigration status in Canada and four years later a citizen.

Faith sometime can test your resilience and resolve to trust God no matter what. The ability to trust God in times of adversity: that is faith. Faith-quantity is not lacking in believers, what is lacking is quality and the patience to wait until God answers. Impatience brings desperation and desperation breeds anxiety, fear and doubt. These if allowed to take root would destroy or cancel our faith. Faith is elastic; stretch it to its elastic limits.

Faith and Unity

Faith works best in unity. It is written "Five of you shall chase a hundred, and a hundred of you shall put ten thousand to flight; your enemies shall fall by the sword before you." Leviticus 26:8

"How could one chase a thousand, And two put ten thousand to flight, unless their Rock had sold them, and the LORD had surrendered them?" Deuteronomy 32:30 "One man of you shall chase a thousand, for the LORD your God is He who fights for you, as He promised you." Joshua 23:10. "Again I say to you that if two of you agree on earth concerning anything that they ask, it will be done for them by My Father in heaven." Matthew 18:19.

The spirit of agreement is the spirit of unity. The spirit of unity is the spirit of faith. The spirit of faith is the spirit of power. The spirit of unity is one not many even if there are more than a hundred people in the agreement. The power of unity is faith raised to the power of the number of people in agreement or 'zexponentially*'; that is, 2^{faith}, 3^{faith}, 10^{faith}, etc. Another way of saying it is: when 3 people are in agreement and each putting in 100% of his/her own faith, the resultant quality of faith available to each of them and to answer their prayer is not 3^3 or 3x3x3 but 100x100x100 or 1,000,000 (1 million) units of faith. The foregoing is an illustration. Faith cannot be measured in any finite instruments.

For this reason unity of faith is so powerful because it is not an addition, multiplication or exponentiation of faith; it is faith

---

*   Zexponentially: Word for infinity of faith coined by the author

raised to 100% in powers by the number of consenting believers or partners. That is what makes the 7ᵗʰ Sense extraordinary and extraordinarily powerful. It can combine zexponentially or infinitely. The scripture says "Till we all come to the unity of the faith and of the knowledge of the Son of God, to a perfect man, to the measure of the stature of the fullness of Christ." Ephesians 4:13.

The 7ᵗʰ Sense combines all the powers and qualities of the other six senses and more. It is power in the spirit and of the spirit. It is for this reason faith is difficult to comprehend completely especially by those whose minds and spirits have not been exercised in the Living Word.

There is tremendous power in unity of faith. Let us not forget the meaning of unit or unity. Unit means one(ness), whole (number), undivided, cord-like or accord in strength, etc. Unity means the state of being one, single-mindedness, perfect harmony, single mind and spirit, total agreement, one accord and so forth. Unity-faith or unity of faith has a lot to do with the collective will, purpose and total agreement of the people. Unit or unity is God because God is One not many. In the building of the Tower of Babel, God looked down and said, "the people is one." "And the LORD said, Behold, the people is one, and they have all one language; and this they begin to do: and now nothing will

be restrained from them, which they have imagined to do."
Genesis11:6 KJV.

The only time that the disciples were in one accord was on the day of Pentecost and the result of it was the unusual release and out pouring of the Holy Ghost in such a dramatic and spectacular manner that heaven was opened and there were visible fire balls or tongues of fire as the Bible called it. "And when the day of Pentecost was fully come, they were all with one accord in one place. And suddenly there came a sound from heaven as of a rushing mighty wind, and it filled the entire house where they were sitting. And there appeared unto them cloven tongues like as of fire, and it sat upon each of them. And they were all filled with the Holy Ghost, and began to speak with other tongues, as the Spirit gave them utterance." Acts 2:1-4. Something unusual and spectacular happens when two or more people meet in the name of the Lord in total and unconditional agreement or one accord. That same spirit of accord probably has never happened again since then. That is the power of unity. It brings down the power of God.

Another place I have read about something resembling a spirit of accord was in Kathryn Khulman's miracle services in the US. The services had such electrifying power that people would begin to receive their healing miracles, sometimes, even before Kathryn herself showed up on stage. The power of the spirit of faith and unity cannot be over-emphasized. It is the power that moves mountains of impossibilities. It makes miracles happen in crusades even in countries with very high non-Christian populations like Pakistan and India as in Peter Youngren's crusades.

Jesus said in Matthew 18:20, "For where two or three are gathered together in my name, there am I in the midst of them." There is no telling of what could happen when two or more believers plus Jesus come together to pray in the spirit of unity and harmony. In Acts 12:1-11, the scripture gave a vivid account of what happened and still could happen when believers come together and pray in unity. It produces what I call Synergy-of-Faith.

Synergy-of-Faith

Synergy-of-Faith is what happens when believers co-operate fully, completely, totally and unconditionally with the Holy Ghost in prayer and in the work of regeneration. Synergy of faith is the co-operative action of two or more believers and the Holy Spirit in any task, prayer or undertaken in the name of Jesus. In such a situation, it is impossible for Satan to resist the power or force produced under such union.

Synergism of faith has to do more with spiritual work, actions and activities related to the preaching of the gospel. It functions when different levels of individual faith coming together and presenting a common purpose to God. In other words, Synergy of faith functions when different individual believers with different levels of faith join together in the Spirit of absolute unity and harmony. When this happens, the combined total faith-energy produced and released, can only be quantified xexponentially but the quality thereof, is like the meeting of angels or the disciples of Jesus without Judas in the upper room at Pentecost, Acts 2:1-4. Another example was when Herod the King planned kill the Apostle Peter in Acts12:1-16.

Peter Delivered from Prison

Now about that time Herod the king stretched out his hand to harass some from the church. [2] Then he killed James the brother of John with the sword. [3] And because he saw that it pleased the Jews, he proceeded further to seize Peter also. Now it was during the Days of Unleavened Bread. [4] So when he had arrested him, he put *him* in prison, and delivered him to four squads of soldiers to keep him, intending to bring him before the people after Passover.

⁵ Peter was therefore kept in prison, but constant prayer was offered to God for him by the church. ⁶ And when Herod was about to bring him out, that night Peter was sleeping, bound with two chains between two soldiers; and the guards before the door were keeping the prison. ⁷ Now behold, an angel of the Lord stood by him, and a light shone in the prison; and he struck Peter on the side and raised him up, saying, "Arise quickly!" And his chains fell off *his* hands. ⁸ Then the angel said to him, "Gird yourself and tie on your sandals"; and so he did. And he said to him, "Put on your garment and follow me."⁹ So he went out and followed him, and did not know that what was done by the angel was real, but thought he was seeing a vision. ¹⁰ When they were past the first and the second guard posts, they came to the iron gate that leads to the city, which opened to them of its own accord; and they went out and went down one street, and immediately the angel departed from him.

¹¹ And when Peter had come to himself, he said, "Now I know for certain that the Lord has sent His angel, and has delivered me from the hand of Herod and from all the expectation of the Jewish people."

¹² So, when he had considered this, he came to the house of Mary, the mother of John whose surname was Mark, where many were gathered together praying. ¹³ And as Peter knocked at the door of the gate, a girl named Rhoda came

to answer.[14] When she recognized Peter's voice, because of her gladness she did not open the gate, but ran in and announced that Peter stood before the gate. [15] But they said to her, "You are beside yourself!" Yet she kept insisting that it was so. So they said, "It is his angel." [16] Now Peter continued knocking; and when they opened the door and saw him, they were astonished.

Unity brings synergy and synergy has powerful spiritual force that no power or force can withstand. Synergy of faith is what the church is fast losing because of internal divisions, strife, rancor and lack of true love within the church hierarchy. Unity of faith resulting in synergy of faith is what the church needs now to carry every member along and finish the work of God in this end time. The bible says, 'so there will be no division in the body.' "That there should be no schism in the body; but that the members should have the same care one for another." 1Corinthians12:25.

Because individual members of the body of Christ is endowed with different spiritual gifts and different levels of faith, when the church comes together in the spirit of love, unity and faith, there will always be an explosive release of spiritual power that can move every mountain. Pastors should stop wanting to go it alone all the time and begin to tap into the power of unity and synergy in order to grow the church spiritually as well as numerically. Synergy of faith requires love, unity and faith.

Faith grows with use; the more you work your faith, your faith works for you. If you neglect to use your faith all the time, it starts to diminish. Faith must constantly be applied to any and every situation to sustain and grow it.

Faith and Grace

The best way to grow your faith is living by grace one day at a time. Living by grace means trusting Jesus or trusting in the name of Jesus. Trusting the name of Jesus can be as simple and uncomplicated as saying or waving his name over every intractable problem that you face. Jesus, Son of the Living God is the basis of all godly faith. If you need instant faith, call Jesus.

If you are experiencing difficulties having faith or growing your faith simply call on the name of Jesus Christ of Nazareth and ask for faith or confidence to use the faith you already have. This kind of faith is not for keeps. It is for action, for immediate application, it is for immediate results. If you are in danger call Jesus. If you are afraid, call Jesus, if you are persecuted, call Jesus. If you have been diagnosed with a terminal disease, call Jesus. If you need salvation call Jesus. If you need peace of mind, call Jesus. If you have no friend and you need someone to comfort you now, call Jesus. But do not call Jesus in vain. It is a sin to call that name in vain or for fun. If you do, you may be in for a big disappointment when you need Him most.

You may be saying 'but I have been calling and nothing is happening.' It is not true, something is happening except you are calling with a wavering faith, impatience, doubt, or wrong motive, etc. You cannot receive anything by faith if you are double minded.

Peter trusted Jesus and instantly walked on water. Blind Bartimaeus trusted Jesus and instantly receive his sight. The woman with a bleeding problem trusted Jesus and received instant healing without Jesus touching her. If you are looking for lost item, ask Jesus. If you forgot your driver's license at home and need protection, call Jesus. If you don't know what to do or are confused call Jesus. If you are suffering call and trust Jesus.

Jesus is the reason for our faith. The faith that Jesus gives is by grace. It is given by grace and received by faith. Your righteousness is not the basis for God's grace; your good work is not required. Your fasting is not necessary as desirable as it is. When you are living by grace, you are living on Christ's mercy, love, compassion, kindness, divine resources, favor, goodness and promises. This is what I call automatic faith. You just simply live on His own faith. However, you must take the step of faith to call His name. Romans 10:14 says, "How shall they call on Him whom they have not believed.

The moment you call, it means you have just activated your faith even if you did not believe previously. The more the emotional energy, trust or faith that you bring or mix with your believing the better the result or response will be even if you have never believed before. Do not exchange emotions for faith. Crying and shaking and shouting while praying is not faith. Faith is believing and trusting God totally and unconditionally. It is more a thing of the spirit than of the physical even though natural faith can be generated by active emotions.

When Jesus asked Peter to come to Him walking on the water, Peter did not step out on his own faith alone to walk on the water, rather on the faith of Jesus also which was contained in the Word that Jesus spoke to him. It was the Word of Jesus that moved Him. Remember Peter and the other disciples were already afraid when they saw Jesus like a ghost walking on the water. However, when Peter took away the eyes of his faith from Jesus and substituted his fear for Jesus' faith, He began to sink. We too can live on/by and in agreement with Jesus' own faith contained in His Word. We can practice using and living by automatic or auto-faith. Auto faith acts on the Word without analyzing. Auto faith is doing God's Word automatically.

"And in the fourth watch [between 3:00-6:00 a.m.] of the night, Jesus came to them, walking on the sea. And when the disciples saw Him walking on the sea, they were terrified and said it is a ghost! And they screamed out with fright.

But instantly He spoke to them, saying, 'take courage I Am' [it is I] Stop being afraid! And Peter answered Him, Lord, if it is You, command me to come to You on the water.

He said, Come! So Peter got out of the boat and walked on the water, and he came toward Jesus. But when he perceived and felt the strong wind, he was frightened, and as he began to sink, he cried out, Lord, save me [from death]!

Instantly Jesus reached out His hand and caught and held him, saying to him, O you of little faith, why did you doubt? And when they got into the boat, the wind ceased. And those in the boat knelt and worshiped Him, saying, Truly You are the Son of God"

Today, Jesus has given us His name and His Word in the place of His person. John 16:23-24. The name of Jesus is very powerful like no other and it is honored in heaven, on earth and under the earth. It is feared in the air, on land and in the sea. Its powers are far reaching beyond the borders of this world. It travels a billion times faster than the speed of light. There is not a problem situation that can stop it. It is incredibly powerful, that is why it is the only name that bears the title, Omnipotent. [Please read also my book: "Authority of the excellent Name of Jesus."]

The grace-faith is the highest kind of faith yet the simplest and easiest to apply to any situation. The lyric of a song says "God said it and I believe it; that settles it for me. Some may doubt that His Word is true; I've chosen to believe it, what about you?" Until we begin to believe without doubting we would not be able to see the fullness of the power of our faith. Like salvation, it is so easy yet many people have problem believing in being born again or being saved. Automatic faith, which is the 7th sense faith, is a gift of grace that every one must receive. It is free and always available just for the asking.

CHAPTER 12

WORD OF FAITH

The Industry of the Word

By this sub-heading I mean, the industries built around the Word of God. Just as the Bible is the best-selling book of all times so are the businesses that revolve around the Word which I call the Industry of the Word.

One of the reasons I so strongly believe in, adhere to and accept the Bible as the Word of God is that down through the ages men and women from every nation where the good news of Jesus Christ and the Word of God has been preached have received and accepted the Word without force and have created industries that have employed million and millions of people directly and indirectly.

Think for a moment the number of churches (industry), pastors, teachers, counselors, departments of Theology, Bible schools, seminaries, publishing houses, administrators, sales people, believers all over the world, authors, billions of books published and being published even as I am writing. Consider the number of people who have read the Bible at one time or the other for whatever reason. Imagine how many copies of the Bible have been printed down through the millennia and those currently in circulation all over the world; (personally I currently own about ten Bibles), not to talk about the ones I have used since I was a child. Remember hundreds of millions of people who have been healed touched, delivered or prayed for, for one reason or another by faith in the Word of God.

Add to these the countless number of songs that have been composed or written which strains came from the words of the Bible; and do not forget the extravagant wealth of the music industry: the singers and artists, the composers and directors, the musical instruments of all sorts in every culture and every nation under heaven. Include the film industry: the actors, directors, businesses, up and down stream industries and utilities. Think of other services and personnel all over the world including cloth and garment industries, tailors, machineries and manufacturers and other outfitters, shoes, woods, carpenters, buildings and builders, wine, oil (especially olive oil). The list is endless of instruments of civilization and human existence that emanated directly or indirectly from the preaching, application and administration of the Word of God.

These all go to show how powerful the Word is and how it has sustained itself down through the centuries and until eternity. The Bible says, "Having been born again, not of corruptible seed but incorruptible, through the word of God which lives and abides forever, because

"All flesh is as grass, and all the glory of man as the flower of the grass. The grass withers, and its flower falls away, but the word of the LORD endures forever." 1 Peter 1:23-25

Faith Story

One of the many times I made a spirited prayer of faith was when I was in high school [secondary school]. It happened that one young man from my village by name Christian was about to travel to England for studies. In those days going abroad was a big thing and the exclusive preserve of the wealthy and well connected. Considering my very humble background, the idea of even going to university had never crossed my mind much more going abroad for studies until the day he was being sent forth in a church service.

I was a regular church goer but knew nothing about faith. However, during the church service something struck inside of me to ask God for an opportunity to study abroad like he gave to that young man. I bowed down my head and with all my heart and all that was within me I ask God for an opportunity like the one He gave to that young man. I prayed very earnestly with that definite desire and nothing more. At the end of it I felt relieved of the burden I had felt earlier on. I felt I was heard and I went home. Five years after graduation from high school, I still couldn't get admission into any Nigerian University despite repeated trials every year for admission. Then I changed my attention from seeking admission into local universities to applying to American Universities abroad and within a couple of weeks the very first university that I applied to responded favorably and eventually offered me admission within months and I found myself later studying abroad just as I had asked for that day at Christian's send-forth service. That episode taught me that directed faith receives divine response always. Targeted prayers and affirmations assure us of heavens response. Faith that brings positive results is the faith that works with other emotions of hope, love, perseverance, desire, definite ideas, definiteness of purpose and actions. Faith never goes wrong or fails. If it is faith, it is faith and cannot go wrong because faith is pure but if the motive is wrong, then the prayer could be delayed.

Weapons of Faith

"Finally, my brethren, be strong in the Lord and in the power of His might. Put on the whole armor of God that you may be able to stand against the wiles of the devil. For we do not wrestle against flesh and blood, but against principalities, against powers, against the rulers of the darkness of this age, against spiritual hosts of wickedness in the heavenly places. Therefore take up the whole armor of God that you may be able to withstand in the evil day, and having done all, to stand."

Stand therefore, having girded your waist with truth, having put on the breastplate of righteousness, and having shod your feet with the preparation of the gospel of peace; above all, taking the shield of faith with which you will be able to quench all the fiery darts of the wicked one. And take the helmet of salvation, and the sword of the Spirit, which is the word of God; praying always with all prayer and supplication in the Spirit, being watchful to this end with all perseverance and supplication for all the saint"
Ephesian 6:10-18.

Weapons of faith are spiritual weapons with which we battle and defend our faith and invariably ourselves from all spiritual attacks. Faith itself is a spiritual force and a spiritual weapon and must be used in conjunction with other spiritual weapons to achieve maximum success especially in spiritual warfare. Spiritual warfare is real, so are spiritual enemies, opponents or oppositions. However, if you do not understand spiritual warfare and spiritual weapons please seek for help or contact this author.

In the above scripture, there are a number of spiritual weapons mentioned. There are other weapons not mentioned here which are also mentioned and used in the scripture. They include the name of Jesus, the blood of Jesus, the Holy Spirit, angelic hosts, prayer of agreement, prayer commands, fasting, praises and worship, speaking in tongues, righteousness, anointing with oil, etc. These and other spiritual weapons are available to the believer.

Faith and Confession

Confession is the outward expression of an inward belief or desire. Unless intentionally done to deceive, your confession expresses or conveys your thought, desire and the amount of faith it carries. Empty words lack faith or enough faith to bring it to pass but powerful words carry enough faith that make them happen or come true. This explains why most of our prayers are not answered. We speak empty words that have no faith-bones [backbone]. Empty prayers that have no faith-bones are powerless to create anything or change anything.

It has been said that confession brings possession, no, not in all cases. Only confessions loaded with power and faith take possession. The scripture says "Truly I tell you, if anyone says to this mountain, 'Go, throw yourself into the sea,' and does not doubt in their heart but believes that what he says will happen, it will be done for him. Therefore I tell you, whatever you ask for in prayer, believe that you have received it, and it will be yours. Mark11:23. NIV.

Another translation renders it this way, "I can guarantee this truth: This is what will be done for someone who doesn't doubt but believes what he says will happen: He can say to this mountain, 'Be uprooted and thrown into the sea,' and it will be done for him. That's why I tell you to have faith that you have already received whatever you pray for, and it will be yours."

This passage does not cease to fascinate me. This is the spiritual basis for prayer and miracles. Let us here analyze this stupendous statement made by Jesus to His disciples. First in Mark 11verse 22, Jesus commanded them to have faith in God. In order words, He was telling them to have God as an anchor, base, rock, backbone or strength for their faith. Jesus recognized that faith does not just fly in the air by chance. He knew that without a firm base their faith would not stand, it would wobble and fail. Jesus could have said to them, Have faith in yourselves. Some of them were strong men and could fight and do great things. But He told them to have faith in God even though they had never seen God with their physical eyes. This is because no one is complete in himself and only God, Faith in God, can move your mountain. Spiritual mountains and strongholds are made and sustained by spiritual powers. Therefore, you would always need stronger spiritual power which only God can provide.

Anyone ever told you to have faith in God? Please don't ignore them, don't dismiss it as jargon or meaningless. He or she has given you a base or an advice for your faith to take off. It is always a timely advice and should be taken seriously and acted upon immediately no matter how many times you hear it. Having faith in God will restore your self confidence, invigorate your mind, increase your inner strength, stabilize your faith and give you peace of mind. As you read this book, please have faith in God no matter what your situation is. God is greater than your mountains.

Then Jesus proceeded to teach them the ever-living truth of all times about faith. He said "I tell you the truth..." What is truth? Truth is an accurate, established and verified fact that cannot be changed. The reason Jesus told them first of all that this statement is true was that He had tested and applied it at different times, in indifferent situations, at different occasions and in different places and the results were the same each time. This truth is a gospel truth. It can never change and it can never fail. Jesus guaranteed it. You can believe it and be rest assured that it will not fail you. If you have failed before, it was not the truth that failed; it was your doubt that failed. Truth never fails, faith never fails, God's Word never fails and Jesus never fails. Doubt, unbelief, fear and anxiety will always fail you.

Yet Another translation says "For verily I say unto you, That whosoever shall say unto this mountain, Be thou removed, and be thou cast into the sea; and shall not doubt in his heart, but shall believe that those things which he saith shall come to pass; he shall have whatsoever he saith. Therefore I say unto you, what things soever ye desire, when ye pray, believe that ye receive them, and ye shall have them." Mark 11:22. KJV

Did Jesus deliberately say "...and shall not doubt in his heart..." or was he just using words? Jesus was very deliberate and intentional when he said it. He knew firsthand that you cannot operate faith and doubt at the same time. One of them must win. This is because doubt has all the circumstantial evidences all around you to make you not to believe your faith. You lost your job and haven't found another yet. You are poor and are struggling to get by. You owe so much you are afraid you might lose your home, you are divorced or your spouse just left you. The doctors have told you that you have a terminal or incurable disease. Your children are not doing well and you are very concerned something bad might happen to them. You have no immigration papers and they are threatening to deport you. I can go on and on and on.

You alone know where the shoe pinches. The Word of Jesus still resonates today. "Have faith In God" And say to the mountain "Be thou removed and be thou cast into the sea and do not doubt" what you say. Then you shall have what you said. Depending on your faith and what you are asking for, you will be blessed and at the first opportunity of divine providence. God is not a man and He does not lie. "God is not human, that he should lie, not a human being, that he should change his mind. Does he speak and then not act? Does he promise and not fulfill?" Numbers 23:19. God is altogether faithful. He will either answer you the way you spoke or asked or He will give you what He knows is best for you except there are other issues militating against you or your prayer. This is where faith works with discernment. Faith and right standing with God [righteousness] also work hand in hand.

Peradventure you do not have a right standing with God or your heart condemns you when you try to approach God. Here is what you should do. Stop trying to approach God on your own. It won't work. God is holy and may not attend to you in your self righteousness. Instead approach Him through His Son Jesus Christ and you will see the difference immediately. Simply say this prayer.

Dear Jesus, I am sorry for my sins. I want to make peace with you today. Please come into my heart and be my Lord and Savior and wash away my sins in your blood and give me access to the throne of Grace so that I may obtain mercy and grace. Thank you for answering my prayer. In your name Jesus Christ of Nazareth I pray. Amen

FAITH SCRIPTURES

1. Romans 10: 17. So then faith comes by hearing, and hearing by the word of God.
2. 2 Corinthians 5:7. For we walk (live) by faith, not by sight.
3. Hebrews 10:38. Now the just shall live by faith; but if anyone draws back, my soul has no pleasure in him."
4. And without faith it is impossible to please God, because anyone who comes to Him must believe that

He exists and that He rewards those who earnestly (diligently) seek him.

5. Mark 9:23: Jesus said to him, "If you can believe, all things are possible to him who believes."

6. John 3:16: For God so loved the world that he gave his one and only (begotten) Son, that whoever believes in him shall not perish but have eternal life.

7. John 5:24: "Very truly I tell you, whoever hears my word and believes Him who sent me has eternal life and will not be judged but has crossed over from death to life.

8. John 11:25: Jesus said to her, "I am the resurrection and the life, he who believes in Me, though he may die, he shall live.

9. And when He (Jesus) had come into the house, the blind men came to Him. And Jesus said to them, "Do you believe that I am able to do this?" They said to Him, "Yes, Lord." Then He touched their eyes, saying, "According to your faith let it be to you. "And their eyes were opened.

10. Mark 5:34. And He (Jesus) said to her, "Daughter, your faith has made you well. Go in peace, and be healed of your affliction."

11. James 2:17-22. Thus also faith by itself, if it does not have works, is dead. But someone will say, "You have faith, and I have works." Show me your faith without your works, and I will show you my faith by

my works. You believe that there is one God. You do well. Even the demons believe—and tremble! But do you want to know, O foolish man, that faith without works is dead? Was not Abraham our father justified by works when he offered Isaac his son on the altar? Do you see that faith was working together with his works, and by works faith was made perfect?

12. Matthew 21:21. So Jesus answered and said to them, "Assuredly, I say to you, if you have faith and do not doubt, you will not only do what was done to the fig tree, but also if you say to this mountain, 'Be removed and be cast into the sea,' it will be done.

13. Mark 11:22-24. So Jesus answered and said to them, "Have faith in God. For assuredly, I say to you, whoever says to this mountain, 'Be removed and be cast into the sea,' and does not doubt in his heart, but believes that those things he says will be done, he will have whatever he says. Therefore I say to you, whatever things you ask when you pray, believe that you receive them, and you will have them.

14. Matthew 17:20: So Jesus said to them, "Because of your unbelief; for assuredly, I say to you, if you have faith as a mustard seed, you will say to this mountain, 'Move from here to there,' and it will move; and nothing will be impossible for you.

15. Matthew 9:2: Then behold, they brought to Him a paralytic lying on a bed. When Jesus saw their faith,

He said to the paralytic, "Son, be of good cheer; your sins are forgiven you."

16. Matthew 14:31: And immediately Jesus stretched out His hand and caught him, and said to him, "O you of little faith, why did you doubt?"

17. Matthew 15:28: Then Jesus answered and said to her, "O woman, great is your faith! Let it be to you as you desire." And her daughter was healed from that very hour.

18. Luke 17:5 And the apostles said to the Lord, "Increase our faith." So the Lord said, "If you have faith as a mustard seed, you can say to this mulberry tree, 'Be pulled up by the roots and be planted in the sea,' and it would obey you.

19. Romans 14:23: "… for whatever *is* not from faith is sin."

20. Galatians 5:6: For in Christ Jesus neither circumcision nor uncircumcision avails anything, but faith working through love.

21. 1John 5:4: For whatever is born of God overcomes the world. And this is the victory that has overcome the world—our faith.

22. 1Corinthians16: 13: Be on your guard; stand firm in the faith; be courageous; be strong.

23. Ephesians 6:16: Above all, taking the shield of faith with which you will be able to quench all the fiery darts of the wicked one.

24. Hebrews 11: 1: Faith assures us of things we expect and convinces us of the existence of things we cannot see.

25. Hebrews 11:1: Now faith is the substance of things hoped for, the evidence of things not seen.

26. Matthew 6:30: Now if God so clothes the grass of the field, which today is, and tomorrow is thrown into the oven, will He not much more clothe you, O you of little faith?

27. James 1:5-6: If any of you lacks wisdom, you should ask God, who gives generously to all without finding fault, and it will be given to you. But when you ask, you must believe and not doubt, because the one who doubts is like a wave of the sea, blown and tossed by the wind.

28. 1Timothy 6:11: But you, man of God, flee from all this, and pursue righteousness, godliness, faith, love, endurance and gentleness.

29. Romans 1:17: … the righteousness of God is revealed from faith to faith; as it is written, "The just shall live by faith."

30. Romans 5: 1: Therefore, since we have been justified through faith, we have peace with God through our Lord Jesus Christ.

31. Philippians 3:9: and be found in Him, not having my own righteousness, which is from the law, but that

which is through faith in Christ, the righteousness which is from God by faith.

32. 2Chronicles 20:20: … they rose early in the morning and went out into the Wilderness of Tekoa; and as they went out, Jehoshaphat stood and said, "Hear me, O Judah and you inhabitants of Jerusalem: Believe in the LORD your God and you shall be established; believe His prophets, and you shall prosper."

33. Daniel 3:17: If that is the case, our God whom we serve is able to deliver us from the burning fiery furnace, and He will deliver us from your hand, O king.

34. Psalms 37:3: Commit your way to the LORD, trust also in Him, and He shall bring it to pass.

35. Psalms 118:8: It is better to trust in the LORD than to put confidence in man.

36. Proverbs 3:5: Trust in the LORD with all your heart, and lean not on your own understanding.

37. Isaiah 26:3: You will keep him in perfect peace, whose mind is stayed on You, because he trusts in You.

"And Shall Not Doubt In His Heart"

This phrase holds the key to unlocking the miracle working power of faith in you. What does it mean not to doubt in your heart? What I have discovered when we say, "I am believing God for this or that" is that we pray and continue to pray thinking that prayer is or equal to faith and believing. Prayer in itself is not faith. Prayer is communication with God. As much as prayer is very good and very desirable, praying with any form of doubt in you mind will cancel or destroy the efficacy of your prayer. Then prayer becomes empty words. Prayer without doubt makes it a powerful weapon and an instrument of possessing what you desire. Do your utmost to remember this phrase "…And shall not doubt in his heart…" Mark 11:23 whenever you are praying.

Doubt is such a subtle emotion that the enemy sows into our hearts after you have prayed and some times, even before you pray. It works in your subconscious to make you focus on yourself, your weaknesses, failures, inadequacies, inabilities, lack, and the hopelessness of your present circumstances and situations. Doubt will make you to focus on the negative side of faith and all the things that can make things go wrong or that will make it impossible for you to receive your desire. Your doubt could discredit the ability, willingness, and holiness of God and the qualifications of the person[s] praying for or with you.

Faith is not in a person or thing. Faith is always in God. That was the reason Jesus first admonished his disciples in Mark 11:22 to "Have faith in God." Faith is a very sensitive emotion. It does not take any significant persuasion for it to fly or withdraw leaving you with a false hope that you still have faith for the things you are hoping to receive. This will leave you with faith that has decreased or degenerated to hope while you are thinking you still believe. The returning of faith to hope is one of the most subtle things I have seen and known in my Christian walk with God. Faith should not be placed on the thing you are hoping for but in the Living God because it is Him alone that will determine when you will receive. We should always examine our faith from time to time. Faith that brings a quick result is a growing faith. If it is not absolute faith, it could be hope.

It does not take much persuasion to sow a seed of doubt where there was once faith. Mind what I have just said. It does not take much persuasion to sow a seed of doubt. Doubt could be sown by a friend, a trusted friend, parents, a fellow Christian, your doctor, a professor or teacher, the media, even your pastor. However, our greatest enemy is our own mind. A mind that is devoid of the Word of God is a breeding ground for all sorts of emotional swing. Faith is a sensitive emotion. If you really want to walk by faith or take on a faith project, you must shut the doors of your mind tightly against any ideas, suggestions, thoughts, imaginations, beliefs and persons that are contrary or that compete with your faith in God. Your faith or the thoughts that support and encourage your faith must be the dominant energy in your mind.

Faith does not tolerate double mindedness. "A double minded person is unstable in all his ways" ... let not that man think that he shall receive any thing from the Lord. A double minded man is unstable in all his ways. James 1:6-8 says

Faith requires a rock-solid stability and that kind of stability is not commonly found in humans. It is mostly resident in/ with God. The more your faith in God grows by the study of the Word of God, the easier it becomes for you to trust Him in times of need and emergency. It is during the times of emergency and extreme circumstances that God tests our faith in Him. Self-doubt and self-unworthiness are among the major destroyers of faith.

The reason we pray too much and receive too little answers is because of doubts and double mindedness. It does not matter whether you are a new believer or a bishop, your faith must be single and anchored in God in order to receive and continue to receive answers to prayers. You should settle the object/subject of your prayer in your mind and agree without equivocation of faith in what you are going to ask or pray for in advance of the prayer. As I mentioned earlier, faith expires as soon as it is applied. The faith of yesterday, no matter how big it was, cannot sustain another prayer or prayer project unless you have attended that level of faith previously. Every new prayer/project must come with a fresh faith.

Timing is vey important in the maintenance or sustenance of your faith. Before you start a prayer-project decide and determine the time frame for that prayer. If it is an immediate need, you may add the word 'now' to that prayer. If it is not so immediate, you should indicate to God exactly the time frame when you expect the answers based on the real need and not just arbitrarily. Let me state here that God is not bound by your time or timing but the time line you give will more than anything else help to keep you focused and your faith propped up throughout the period of prayer and waiting.

I Believe, Help My Unbelief.

And He (Jesus) asked the scribes, "What are you discussing with them?" Then one of the crowds answered and said, "Teacher, I brought You my son, who has a mute (dumb) spirit. And wherever it seizes him, it throws him down; he foams at the mouth, gnashes his teeth, and becomes rigid. So I spoke to Your disciples, that they should cast it out, but they could not." He answered him and said, "O faithless generation, how long shall I be with you? How long shall I bear with you? Bring him to Me. Then they brought him to Him. And when he [the spirit] saw Him [Jesus], immediately the spirit convulsed him, and he fell on the ground and wallowed, foaming at the mouth. So He asked his father, "How long has this been happening to him?"

And he said, "From childhood. And often he has thrown him both into the fire and into the water to destroy him. But if You can do anything, have compassion on us and help us." Jesus said to him, "If you can believe, all things are possible to him who believes." Immediately the father of the child cried out and said with tears, "Lord, I believe; help my unbelief!" Mark 9:16-24.

The man in the above scripture confronted his own unbelief and doubts by asking Jesus the Master and Author of our faith to help his faithlessness and Jesus did and healed his child. There is no reason pretending that you have enough faith when you do not. There is no need in making people to believe in you when you do not believe in yourself. It is pride and the scripture says that "Pride goes before destruction and a haughty spirit before a fall." Proverbs 16:18. If you know or think that you do not have faith or not enough faith, ask God. Tell it to Jesus. He will help you. Scripture says, anyone who lacks wisdom, should ask from God who gives generously or liberally and without reproach and it will be given him. James 1:5. The same goes for faith. When we lack adequate faith to tackle a situation, we should immediately ask God for an infilling of our faith with the spirit of faith. It works. One of the 9 gifts of the Holy Spirit in 1Corinthians 12:9 is faith.

Faith does not work with pride. Faith does not come by the many high sounding and empty words that we preachers use to show the level of our erudition and faith. The many hours of prayers and fasting that we put in does not move God or change any thing if there is not adequate faith commensurate with the petition you are making. Daniel prayed for 21 days and his prayer was answered the very first day he began. Daniel 10:12.

There were other militating factors to that prayer delays but the point I am making here is that any prayer mixed with adequate amount or level of faith will receive immediate answers. It is at the point of adequate faith level that our prayers get answered. The same is true when we go to buy things with money. It is not until you have paid the exact amount of money for a priced item before it can be yours. As money is the medium of exchange in the physical world so is faith in the spirit realms.

There Are No 'Ifs' With Faith

There are no "Ifs" with faith. It is either faith or no faith. An 'If' is a word that connotes doubt, conditionality, uncertainty, insecurity, unbelief, lack of confidence, and lack of absolute trust. It connotes unsettled questions such as: Is it the will of God to heal me? Can I trust God alone? Can God meet this deadline? What if He fails? How can I be sure? I can't, I'm worried and a host of other negative thoughts and concerns that provide a double mindedness which take away the single mindedness of faith.

'If" is a word that must be discarded and rejected in its entirety when dealing with faith. It is the word Satan uses to sows seeds of doubt, fear, unbelief, anxiety and lack of faith in our hearts. 'If' is a small but mighty word that robs us of our faith and its benefits. Whenever you are in doubt concerning God's Word or you faith, say out loud, Lord I believe but please help my unbelief.

You should always be sensitive in the spirit when praying and when considering a faith project. Let us remove the word 'if' from our faith vocabulary and replace it with the word 'when.' Then you will be saying things like: when God answers my prayer; when God heals me or when I am healed; when I pass my exam, etc. These are some words that encourage faith and expectation. Faith is always forward looking and expectant. You can not be applying faith without expecting and seeing results.

Living by Faith

Living and walking by faith means being filled with the knowledge of the Word of God, acting and speaking by the authority of the word of faith. There is an enormous power stored in the Word of God than anyone of us would ever know. It is the power of Heaven. It is the power with which God made this universe. That power has been delegated to us but is only accessible through faith in the Word. Study the Word to build your capacity for faith action. The stronger your faith, the easier it is for you and me to do spectacular and extraordinary things in word and deed. I am not trying to tickle your fancy. I am telling you the gospel truth as was revealed to me. All the military powers in this world cannot stand the power of the Word of God. But we are impotent and sometimes helpless in the face of such a stupendous power that is available to us. This is so sad.

Living by faith means to appropriate your faith to your daily situations. However, most people wrongly interpret and misappropriate the Word of God and think that being a man or woman of faith is equivalent to financial prosperity. Living by faith is living by the sufficiency which God supplies. Most people who lived by faith were not poor beggars but most of them intentionally shunned affluence and financial gains, because they understood that the love of money is the greatest distraction the devil has in his arsenal. Those who live by faith live on a different and higher spiritual level and therefore, see life very differently from the majority of us. Everyone who lives and walks by faith will always have all his needs met and will be joyful, satisfied and contented. More importantly, they live closer to God.

Word of Faith

What is word of faith? Word of faith is a power-full, motivating, fearless, doubtless utterance from an individual who believes in the efficacy, supremacy and the creative abilities of what he says. Faith always finds expression in spoken words and actions. Word of faith could be a prayer, an affirmation, a decree, a preaching, prophesy, word of wisdom or word of knowledge. It is a powerful confession when you are in the spirit and you are moved and motivated by the spirit. Word of faith impacts lives and brings results and solves problems.

As seen above, faith is belief, confidence, conviction, credence, credit, dependence, optimism, complete trust, assurance, persuasion, confirmation, reality, proof, evidence, certainty, etc. Faith makes you to be sure that you will get what you are asking.

Faith is the knowing that what we hope for and what we expect to happen will happen as we expect it or even better. Faith boosts and solidifies our confidence. It is the unseen factor that consolidates and solidifies our hopes and expectations and brings them into reality.

Faith is a strong conviction with internal evidence of something for which there may be no tangible physical proof of its existence but there is a knowing within you that it exists. It is complete trust in and devotion to the existence of possibilities in the unseen worlds. Faith is more than believing, it is a source of power. Faith means trusting God to do what might never have been seen, heard or done before. So faith focuses on the promises given in God's Word and the reality and ability of the creative powers with the believer.

Most of us operate faith unconsciously and that is the reason we are not always sure whether our prayers will be answered or not. But faith should be operated consciously and intentionally. This book is about getting us to begin to operate in Conscious-Faith. Conscious-faith is the ability to use our faith intentionally, deliberately and purposefully to achieve God's divine purposes. There is the element of knowing that most of us ignore or are not cognizant of about faith. Faith is a spiritual sense and like all other senses we can use it intentionally.

Faith is the conscious ability to see or conceive something in the spirit and deliberately and intentionally bring it to physical reality. That is calling those things which are not seen as if you are already seeing them. This is taking your faith to a new and higher level. This higher level requires faith and practice. It is not gained overnight but is absolutely possible.

There is another world, a real world, as real as our own world where everything is possible and available. This world is called the faith-world or spirit world. In this world you can do anything and get anything you want or desire. In that world nothing dies, nothing changes, nothing is impossible and nothing is foolishness. Faith and imagination will create and give you anything you desire. If you can imagine it, believe it, and pay the price, you will have.

CHAPTER 13

FAITH IN DIFFERENT VERSIONS

Hebrews 11:1:

"Now faith is the substance of things hoped for, the evidence of things not seen." King Jams Version.

"Now faith is confidence in what we hope for and assurance about what we do not see." New International Version.

"Now faith means putting our full confidence in the things we hope for, it means being certain of things we cannot see." J.B. Phillips (New Testament).

"Faith is being sure of what we hope for. It is being certain of what we do not see." NIV Readers Version.

"Faith is the reality of what we hope for, the proof of what we don't see." Common English Bible.

"Faith makes us sure of what we hope for and gives us proof of what we cannot see." Contemporary English Version.

"Faith assures us of things we expect and convinces us of the existence of things we cannot see." God's Word Translation.

"Faith is what makes real the things we hope for. It is proof of what we cannot see." Easy-To-Read Version.

"To have faith is to be sure of the things we hope for, to be certain of the things we cannot see." Good News Translation.

"Now faith is the reality of what is hoped for, the proof of what is not seen." Holman Christian Standard Bible.

"Faith means being sure [the assurance; *or* the tangible reality; *or* the sure foundation] of the things we hope for and knowing that something is real even if we do not see it [the conviction/assurance/evidence about things not seen]. Expanded Bible.

"Now faith is being sure we will get what we hope for. It is being sure of what we cannot see." New Life Version.

"If people believe God, then they know they have the things they hope to get. It is the proof of things we do not see" Worldwide English (New Testament).

"Faith is the assurance of things you have hoped for, the absolute conviction that there are realities you've never seen." The Voice.

"Now faith is the assurance (the confirmation, the title deed) of the things [we] hope for, being the proof of things [we] do not see *and* the conviction of their reality [faith perceiving as real fact what is not revealed to the senses]. Amplified Bible.

Faith is the confidence that what we hope for will actually happen; it gives us assurance about things we cannot see. New living Translation.

Faith Quotations

Genesis 15: 6. And he believed the LORD, and he counted it to him as righteousness.

Ephesians 6:16. In all circumstances take up the shield of faith, with which you can extinguish all the flaming darts of the evil one;

Ephesians 2:8-9. For by grace you have been saved through faith. And this is not your own doing; it is the gift of God, not a result of works, so that no one may boast.

Matthew 8:26. And he said to them, "Why are you afraid, O you of little faith?" Then he rose and rebuked the winds and the sea, and there was a great calm.

Matthew 14:29-31. He said, "Come." So Peter got out of the boat and walked on the water and came to Jesus. But when he saw the wind, he was afraid, and beginning to sink he cried out, "Lord, save me." Jesus immediately reached out his hand and took hold of him, saying to him, "O you of little faith, why did you doubt?"

Matthew 17:20 He said to them, "Because of your little faith. For truly, I say to you, if you have faith like a grain of mustard seed, you will say to this mountain, 'Move from here to there,' and it will move, and nothing will be impossible for you."

Luke 12:27-28. Consider the lilies, how they grow: they neither toil nor spin, yet I tell you, even Solomon in all his glory was not arrayed like one of these. But if God so clothes the grass, which is alive in the field today, and tomorrow is thrown into the oven, how much more will he clothe you, O you of little faith! (Jesus speaking)

Matthew 9:22. Jesus turned, and seeing her he said, "Take heart, daughter; your faith has made you well." And instantly the woman was made well.

Matthew 15:28. Then Jesus answered her, "O woman, great is your faith! Be it done for you as you desire." And her daughter was healed instantly.

John 5:24. Truly, truly, I say to you, whoever hears my word and believes him who sent me has eternal life. He does not come into judgment, but has passed from death to life.

Romans 10:17. So faith comes from hearing, and hearing through the word of Christ.

John 8:24. I told you that you would die in your sins, for unless you believe that I am he you will die in your sins."

1 John 5:1

Everyone who believes that Jesus is the Christ has been born of God, and everyone who loves the Father loves whoever has been born of him.

Faith and Time

Faith works with time. Faith is not indefinite. Faith is time bound. Faith is definite. When you exercise endless faith, you are actually exercising hope. Hope goes on to eternity but faith is for now. Faith works with time after which it expires and lapses to hope. For this reason we must deliberately and consciously set a faith-time for a particular faith project. I must warn here again that faith time is for the active sustenance of your faith. The time is not to pressure God into submission but to help us maintain actively focused faith during the period of your faith project. Faith project could be prayer project, business project, financial project, church project, etc.

When the object of faith is not realized at the expiration of the faith-time or project time, we can reengage another faith-time. In this way our faith is always current and strong. Faith-time is as important to the overall concept of faith as is confidence, belief and assurance, etc. Because faith is a thing of the now, the time element should be considered very seriously.

Faith is always a renewable commodity, therefore if it expires, you renew and reactivate it. That is what is meant in the scripture," The just shall live by faith. Constantly leaving in a new and renewed faith makes you a 'Hot' believer. It makes you ready at all times. The enemy can not mess with you because you are on the cutting edge of faith. You know your rights and privileges in Christ and you know how to use your faith- power. Time is very important in faith application.

Faith and Fasting

One of the strongest builders of faith is fasting. The Word of God and prayer mixed with fasting are faith growers and faith motivators. These three are the power base of a faith life. Unfortunately believers are not taught early enough the virtues of fasting as a vital necessity of a strong and vibrant faith and Christian life.

Fasting is the cleansing agent of the spirit, soul and body. It is written, Having, therefore, these promises, dearly beloved, let us cleanse ourselves from all filthiness of the flesh and spirit, perfecting holiness in the fear of God. 2Corinthians 7:1. The cleansing agent is fasting. And when fasting is applied to the cleansing blood of Jesus they bring about the holiness that God requires to do a quick work in our lives. Not that the blood of Jesus is insufficient of its own but God requires a level of holiness on our part so as not to make the blood of Jesus of non-effect. Fasting is also required to raise our level of faith and purity. Fasting of itself does not move God but it places us in a better position to come into his presence more acceptably to present and receive our petitions through Jesus Christ.

Fasting is a very powerful faith instrument. It helps us organize and take stock of our spiritual lives. It sharpens our 7th Sense and with prayer drives out the demons that enforce besetting sins and weaknesses in our lives. When we are purified through fasting, and our lives become pleasing to the Lord, then whatever we ask believing comes easier than without it. Fasting is highly recommended and in fact is a must for every Christian of all ages. Children should be thought how to fast from infancy so that they will grow with the knowledge and practice of proper fasting. Not all fasting is acceptable to God. Hear what the spirit of God says here.

"Shout it aloud, do not hold back. Raise your voice like a trumpet. Declare to my people their rebellion and to the descendants of Jacob their sins.[2] For day after day they seek me out; they seem eager to know my ways, as if they were a nation that does what is right and has not forsaken the commands of its God. They ask me for just decisions and seem eager for God to come near them. [3] 'Why have we fasted,' they say, 'and you have not seen it? Why have we humbled ourselves, and you have not noticed?' "Yet on the day of your fasting, you do as you please and exploit all your workers. ⁴ Your fasting ends in quarreling and strife, and in striking each other with wicked fists

You cannot fast as you do today and expect your voice to be heard on high. ⁵ Is this the kind of fast I have chosen, only a day for people to humble themselves? Is it only for bowing one's head like a reed and for lying in sackcloth and ashes?

Is that what you call a fast, a day acceptable to the LORD? ⁶ "Is not this the kind of fasting I have chosen: to loose the chains of injustice and untie the cords of the yoke, to set the oppressed free and break every yoke? ⁷ Is it not to share your food with the hungry and to provide the poor wanderer with shelter when you see the naked, to clothe them, and not to turn away from your own flesh and blood?

⁸ Then your light will break forth like the dawn, and your healing will quickly appear; then your righteousness will go before you, and the glory of the LORD will be your rear guard. ⁹ Then you will call, and the LORD will answer; you will cry for help, and he will say: Here am I. Isaiah 58:1-9

This passage lets us know that not all fasting is acceptable before God. Fasting when done properly honors God and brings down the favor of God to bear on our situations. Fasting is very desirable and profitable to all. Fasting is not an optional Christian practice it is an essential faith grower and a power booster for every child of God without exceptions. So learn it and practice it as a vital necessity of spiritual power and warfare.

Faith and Forgiveness

What is forgiveness? Forgiveness is giving unconditional pardon for sin, hurt, and shortcomings of others against you. It is letting go of the hurts of the past and removing the pain from your heart and consciousness. Faith works with a clean and clear conscience. One of the reasons why faith is not working for some is the presence of un-confessed sins, bitterness and un-forgiveness. The presence of these three will leave you in the peripheries of the throne room of God. Un-forgiveness robs you of the confidence God requires in the application of faith. Un-forgiveness destroys deep and intimate relationship with God and makes your faith of less effect. Un-forgiveness on our part can hinder God from forgiving us of our own sins Mark 11: 25-26. And whenever you stand praying, if you have anything against anyone, forgive him and let it drop (leave it, let it go), in order that your Father Who is in heaven may also forgive you your [own] failings and shortcomings and let them drop.

But if you do not forgive, neither will your Father in heaven forgive your failings and shortcomings.

On the other hand, forgiveness restores confidence and vibrant relationship with both God and man and creates the atmosphere conducive for the exercise of faith and godly relationships. Confidence and clear conscience are key ingredients in the exercise and application of faith. Therefore, whatever can rob you of your confidence can also rob you of your faith.

Forgiveness and a clear conscience before God are priceless in His sight and are the keys to maintaining an ever-increasing faith. Some people find it difficult to forgive and put away the hurt. They keep hurting themselves even after they say they have forgiven. Something is wrong somewhere and somehow. Forgiveness is meant to remove the hurt and enmity and produce peace in the heart of the believer. However, forgiveness does not necessarily mean you must go back and be hurt again and again.

CHAPTER 14

WEALTH ACCUMULATION

No one can begin to accumulate large sums of money or wealth until he begins to tap into the rich resource of his creative faith or 7th Sense. No one can rise to his highest level of achievement until he begins to access the powers of his spiritual and creative faith. Everyone is gifted with certain tendencies or propensities to do certain things proficiently and naturally. Therein lies the secret of success and the power or source of wealth accumulation. It takes power-full faith to accumulate wealth, but that power may not necessarily be physical power. It is the power of/in your faith; faith in your gifts and abilities and faith in your creative self. Remember, we have already said that faith is power and faith has power.

The power of life and the power of success and achievement lie buried within your faith. The scripture says" "And you shall remember the LORD your God, for *it is* He who gives you power to get wealth, that He may establish His covenant which He swore to your fathers, as it is this day." Deuteronomy

8:18. That covenant was a covenant of faith. Scripture says that Abraham believed God and it was counted to him as righteousness.

God gives the power; you receive it by grace through faith. The power could be wisdom, physical, mental, spiritual, and all other wealth producing abilities. But none of these could manifest fully without your using or investing your faith power. That is even more important than financial and physical investments one makes. No one can succeed in any venture until he believes he can through faith. There is more hope of success for a poor man of humble means than the son of a rich man that has no faith in his father's line of business. Even when there is an already accumulated wealth, faith is required to apply or employ them to profitable ventures or to keep it from wasting.

Everyone is potentially rich or wealthy. Nature has equipped us equally with one thing, faith. The faith you received at birth is exactly all the faith you will need to attain your highest potential. The faith that Mr. 'A' received could be more or less than Mr. 'B', that is because Mr. 'B's assignment is different from Mr. 'A's. Everyone's gifting and the measure of faith to achieve his own purpose is different. For that reason no one should envy another and everyone should seek and endeavor to find out their purpose(s) early in life and pursue it. However, no time is too late to discover or put your lately discovered faith to work.

When you discover your calling and purpose, life becomes easy and simple and wealth accumulation becomes a source of joy with peace of mind and pleasure. Everyone has faith to succeed. Everyone has power to achieve but not everyone is working in their natural calling with the faith they received. As long as you are in the wrong vocation you may not easily succeed with joy and gladness. Even if you succeed in the alternative field it would always be with much struggles, much overtime (hard work), and much pain.

The invisible resource of the Divine is infinite and inexhaustible. No one who taps into it can say I couldn't find enough resources. It is only in the physical realms that resources are limited and men are struggling for the few things they can see. But the things that cannot be perceived with the five senses are far more than all the wisdom of the world put together can fathom.

"For since the creation of the world His invisible attributes are clearly seen, being understood by the things that are made, *even* His eternal power and Godhead, so that they are without excuse, because, although they knew God, they did not glorify Him as God, nor were thankful, but became futile in their thoughts, and their foolish hearts

were darkened. Professing to be wise, they became fools."
Romans 1:20-22.

You Are Richer Than You Think

You are richer that you think if only you will stop farming/
working in another man's farm and start harvesting your
own over ripe and over grown farm. Many of us are working
other people's jobs, occupying other people's positions on
the jobs that do not require us to use our faith or creative
abilities. All of us are given creative abilities but most of us
are not using ours. If every one of us would find our true
niches in life, there will be order, wealth, contentment and
less evil, envy and heartaches in the world.

Your natural fields are hidden beneath your faith. Many of
us our jobs have become sources of curse and sin because
the scripture say, whatever is not of faith is sin. Roman's
14:23. This reason explains why many people are unhappy
with their jobs and are not prospering. Those who prosper
sincerely and honestly must of necessity have discovered
their callings and niches in life.

You are potentially a rich or wealth person. I know this
would sound foreign to most people reading this book. I
repeat you are far richer than you think. Wealth is in your

spiritual DNA. But because you cannot read your spiritual DNA with your physical senses, you cannot discover it until you begin to walk in the spirit by faith. That does not mean that all of us who claim to be walking in the spirit are walking by our 7th Sense or have the knowledge of assessing and diagnosing our Spiritual DNA. Every thing you need to succeed in this life is already in you as you read. Time and old age cannot change it. You will start prospering the moment you discover and start working with your faith in your destined vocation.

Know this that many of us will need to create our own wealth through faith and wisdom. By now it would be obvious that those who create something new or improve on an already existing thing through the imaginations of their faith, find success much easier than those who job on other people's farms. There is the creative element of God in you, use it. You can be creative as a cook, teacher, dancer, preacher, traffic officer, driver and so forth if you are convinced that that is what you are called to do/be. Every vocation has its own wealth and those who are wealthy in their vocations do so because they have discovered and tapped into the geniuses within them. Every one is a genius whether you believe it or not. If you don't believe it, you will never be one. You are a genus if you will work in the area of your calling. Jesus said, "…be it unto you according to your faith. Matthew 9:29. You cannot rise above the limits you set on your faith.

Remember faith sees the invisible, believes the incredible, touches the untouchable, hears the inaudible, does the unthinkable, writes the indescribable, stops the unstoppable, reaches the unreachable, thinks the impossible, and communicates with the Infinite. Your faith will make you whatever you want to be. It is not late yet. There is no time limitation in the Divine mind. "All things are possible to him that believes." Believe in yourself that you can and believe in God that He is more than able. Then work on what you believe and believe what you work. You are richer than you think and you are worth more than you will ever know. Start now to put that desire, plan and idea into action. You will never know what will happen until you begin to act.

Your 7th Sense holds the key to your prosperity and blessing. Faith is the beginning of all wealth accumulation. Faith gives power and momentum to your seemingly ordinary idea, plan, thought and imagination. It makes them become unstoppable wealth producing things. Do not neglect the small intangible and invisible powers of your faith. They are priceless and worth more than gold if you can harness them. The scripture says "Do not despise these small beginnings, ..." Zechariah 4:10.

Faith is the beginning of all wealth accumulation and achievement and the absence of it is the beginning and end of all failures. It is faith that will make a man rise up when he falls. It is faith that will make a person try again and again or even start all over again after a terrible mishap. It is only faith that will make a man into something or someone he believes to be. However, there are many who don't want to venture into the realms of the unknown. They are content to live in the past. If you are such a person, wake up. Without faith you can never have a miracle no matter how many years you fast. Miracles are the provisions of faith. If you have faith, you will always have miracles in every area of your life, health, finances and all. Miracles could be the daily little things that lubricate the wheel and engine of life or could be the mind-blowing, earth-shaking events of life.

Poorer Than Imagined

You are poorer than you now know if you have a low faith; low self esteem, low self confidence and little or no faith in God. A person with a low self esteem is short changing himself or herself, because he has no faith to present and represent himself. A low self confidence will make you shy, fearful, fault-finding, questioning and often removed or withdrawn from others. It will rob you of fullness of joy and peace and thereby making you critical of others, angry and sometimes envious of those who are rather more confident than you are (maybe not in all cases).

If you have a low confidence of yourself, you could as well be suffering from personal insecurity and inferiority complex thereby robbing yourself of the joy of mixing with the 'college' of good people. If you have a low confidence in yourself, you give people the impression that you cannot be trusted, thereby making them doubt your sincerity even when you are hundred and ten percent honest and sincere. You reduce yourself to a wimp rather that the champion that you are. This is in addition to the physical and financial poverty that you could experience as a result of your low faith or low self-worth. Your self-worth is far more valuable than money. A man's true measure of success in life does not consist in the abundance of things he possesses but in his faith-power and self esteem or self worth. Scripture says "And He said to them, "Take heed and beware of covetousness, for one's life does not consist in the abundance of the things he possesses." Luke 12:15

A low self image or self confidence can make your total self-worth far lower than you had imagined. For the same reason I said you could be poorer than you imagined. The truth is your intrinsic self energy (faith), which actually makes you who you are and gives you a vibrant and radiant energy and positive personality, could be grossly depleted if you live long in self defeat. Your faith and self energy is worth far more that the millions in the bank. There are some poor people who are far more admirable, loveable and attractive than riches can buy. Your faith gives you favor before God and man. There is an amazing grace in faith.

Incredible Statistics

There was a time I tried my hands on the insurance business through Primerica. One of the things they showed us was what I called the incredible statistics. We were taught that insurance companies used Social Security Administration data that revealed how an average person finishes up after retiring from active work-life.

The statistics of a 100 people who have worked for 45 years, from 20 years of age to the retirement age of 65. They would end up as follows:

1 person makes it to the top income brackets and becomes wealthy

4 people would become financially independent and self sufficient

5 persons would still be working

28 people would be dead

62 people would be dead broke or living dead financially

This statistics computed in percentages could be interpreted this way: Only 1% (one percent) of people would be wealthy after working for others for 45 years, 4% (four percent) would be financially rich and comfortable and 95% (ninety-five percent) would be either dead or financially broke. Isn't this incredible? I believe the above statistics could have changed by now because more young people are becoming rich and living longer.

If this statistics were true it meant that only five out of a hundred people did step out and took daring steps of faith to discover and align themselves to their true calling or vocation. I have always believed that money follows every good idea. It means that a lot of people would never discover the powers within them, that is, the power of faith to change or fulfill their destinies. This statistics applied to believers as well as those who do not believe anything. Does it mean that the interpretation of our theology on faith is wrong or is the problem with individual application of the Word?

Scriptures are replete with examples of men and women who did exploits by faith and there are millions of others even in contemporary times that are stepping out of these statistics and are becoming millionaires and others have fulfilled their destinies without being financially very rich. I believe that we are richer than we think and we all have the capacity to change or actualize our own destinies. I believe that after reading this book you will have enough faith-information to do things differently for yourself and pass on the knowledge to others.

The difference between those who get financially rich and those who do not lies in the way each category thinks, uses their 7th Sense and applying faith-action to their thoughts and plans. That includes my humble self. Everyone thinks good thoughts and everyone makes good plans but not everyone applies the necessary and required faith-action to actualize their dreams. This is because most people do not understand the role and importance of faith in the accumulation of wealth.

There cannot be any accumulation of wealth in large quantities without the application of faith. The bottom line question is do you follow up your good thoughts and plans with faith-filled-actions? Without faith it is impossible to prosper. As faith without work is dead so also plan without faith-action is equally dead. Let us begin to work on our faith. Let us begin to faith our plans and work our faith.

CHAPTER 15

FAITH FOR DIFFICULT TIMES

There is faith for all situations that confront you. Many people especially those going through challenges and hard times; do not understand how much they need faith to pull through. You need faith in times of adversity and in good times; whether it is financial problems, sickness and ill health, loss of love or loved ones, loss of business and disasters, retirement without sufficient savings or income, family and marriage problems, you name it. Your greatest resource in times of adversity is your faith. Lose it and you lose your bearing, confidence and the ability and strength to fight on and hope.

Faith is the first responder in times of trouble and adversity. It is your faith in yourself and particularly in your God that pulls you together, sustains you and raises up a pillar of hope for you. In times of adversity, faith and hope are your pillars of strength and comfort. When all hope (old hope) is gone and there is nothing more to look forward to, your faith, if you have any, will raise up a standard against the menacing challenges of the storms before you. Every one of us will face at least one major challenge and about ten minor problems in our life time. For some it will be far greater.

Regardless of the challenge you face you need faith to pull through successfully without much damage and hurt to yourself and others. The scripture says "No test or temptation that comes your way is beyond the course of what others have had to face. All you need to remember is that God will never let you down; he'll never let you be pushed past your limits; he'll always be there to help you come through it." The Message Bible. Another translation puts it this way, "No temptation has overtaken you except such as is common to man; but God is faithful, who will not allow you to be tempted beyond what you are able, but with the temptation will also make the way of escape, that you may be able to bear it." 2 Corinthians 10:13. NKJV.

In times of trouble, you can depend on God through faith but if you have no faith then it will be harder for you to checkmate the tsunami of life and all other forces coming against you from different directions. The first thing that happens when trouble strikes is the loss of faith, loss of self confidence and hope. With these come, confusion, frustration, unbearable stress and fear. For these reasons people breakdown, faint, develop all kinds of sicknesses, low self image, etc., which some never recover from till death and some die early out of heartbreak.

Absolute faith in God brings or restores hope; no matter the circumstance or situation. Faith works with hope. When all hope is gone, if you still believe, then the automatic-faith will kick in to support and sustain your spirit from being crushed, injured or terribly wounded because of the attack you are going through. Some people instead of asking God to increase their faith in times of trouble they begin to ask such faith destroying questions as "'God why me?' What have I done?"

These types of questions when your faith is under attack are self- justifying and self-righteous questions and will only serve to deplete your faith the more. It is better by faith to say I thank you God for this situation even though I don't understand the reason for this situation, I know that by faith I will overcome. Faith is one of the seven pillars that sustain our human existence. Others are hope, peace, joy, love, patience and resilience. In times of trouble our prayer should be, God please increase my faith and let me know that you are still and always with me.

Many people do not think and talk about faith until disaster strikes. People think that faith is only a religious word, but they are dead wrong. Faith is a life support, life sustainer, life builder, and a present help in time of trouble. No matter the type of trouble you are in, faith will sustain you and help you to pull through. It will lift you above the heights of the adversity and actually could turn the adversity into a pleasant opportunity for growth and learning experience. Anyone who loses complete faith in times of adversity like a fatal accident, terminal illness such as cancer, war or stock market crash, etc., might not survive it for long.

Faith is a powerful commodity that is given to us to help preserve our lives, give it momentum and stability. Faith, hope and patience are what you need in times of adversity. They are always complementary to each other. It is high time we started building and nourishing our faith so it can nourish us when difficult times come. The scripture says, "…and this is the victory that overcomes the world, even our faith." 1John 5:4. We do not pray for adversity but they do sometimes come unannounced, unexpected and when we are unprepared. Living by faith prepares you for any eventualities of life.

Here is a poem I that found in the book of Ecclesiastes. It talks about days of adversity and difficulty, what you should do before then.

Remember now your Creator in the days of your youth,
Before the difficult days come,

And the years draw near when you say,
"I have no pleasure in them":

²While the sun and the light,
The moon and the stars,
Are not darkened,
And the clouds do not return after the rain;

³ In the day when the keepers of the house tremble,
And the strong men bow down;
When the grinders cease because they are few,
And those that look through the windows grow dim;

⁴ When the doors are shut in the streets,
And the sound of grinding is low;
When one rises up at the sound of a bird,
And all the daughters of music are brought low.

⁵ Also they are afraid of height,
And of terrors in the way;
When the almond tree blossoms,
The grasshopper is a burden,
And desire fails.
For man goes to his eternal home,
And the mourners go about the streets.

⁶ Remember your Creator before the silver cord is loosed,

Or the golden bowl is broken,
Or the pitcher shattered at the fountain,
Or the wheel broken at the well.
[7] Then the dust will return to the earth as it was,
And the spirit will return to God who gave it.

[8] "Vanity of vanities," says the Preacher,
"All is vanity." Ecclesiastes 12:1-8

The Faithfulness of God

What is faithfulness?

The Webster's Encyclopedic Unabridged Dictionary of the English Language defines faithfulness as "Strict and thorough in the performance of duty. True to ones word, promises, vows, etc. steady in allegiance or affection. Reliable, trusted or believed, true to the fact, original, full of faith (or faith-full), believing, etc.

The Oxford College Thesaurus explains faithfulness as "fidelity, loyalty, constancy, devotion, dependability, reliability, trustworthiness, staunchness, steadfastness, obedience, dedication, commitment, allegiance, etc. These are powerful phrases and words that describe the person and character of God.

Our God is the God of faith. God is faith-full. All faith proceeds from Him and without Him there is and would be no faith or basis for faith. God is faith-full and He requires it from all who come to Him. This is because He has decided to make Himself invisible and incommunicado through any other means. Faith is the only means by which humans can reach God and communicate with Him on a personal and intimate level. But He has also made Himself very assessable if we approach Him by His approved means of communication, our faith. Because He is the only source of faith, He is ever ready to recharge our faith battery whenever we run out or are run down. Because God is a personal being with emotions like ours, He sees how we feel and is compassionate and ready always to fill our faith-tank so we can continue to run well even in the face of all odds and adversities of life.

God is faithful, absolutely faithful, completely trustworthy, incomprehensibly caring and justifiably truthful and committed to His Word. He will not let you down without letting himself down and without making himself a liar and, therefore, no less than a mortal being. The thing that makes Him God is not only that He has all the powers in heaven and earth. What makes Him God is that He is forever faithful to His Word to fulfill, perform and actualize it. Has He said it? It is as good as done. His faithfulness to His Word is what endears Him to humans and angels alike.

God said "…I am watching to see that my word is fulfilled it." Jeremiah 1:12.

We cannot talk about faith without thinking and considering the faithfulness of the God. Faith is the lifeline of all humans. Faith is the only connecting link between man and God. The absence of it will throw our lives into a constant state of fear, instability, doubt, unbelief and spiritual struggles and confusion. When you struggle with faith, you also struggle with insatiability, lack of peace, loss of joy, irritability, spiritual instability and oscillating mood changes. When you lose faith, you also lose self-confidence and self-esteem. Faith is too important to human existence that I consider ignorance of it as life's error of fatalistic proportion. Your life will run even better, no matter how good it is now, if you add faith and more faith to it.

CHAPTER 16

CONFIDENT PERSONALITY

Faith is an absolute confidential trust in God's abilities through you. Faith works with confidence. Faith is manifested in, by, and through confidence in yourself and in God. A true test of faith is the confidence and conviction you possess and exercise when applying faith. There is no fear in faith. There is no faith in doubt. All there is to faith is a completely undivided trust and confidence you present when executing your faith action whether in word or deed. Faith without absolute conviction and true confidence is useless, empty, boasting, proud, powerless, and presumptuous. It will produce no result. Confidence in one's self and natural abilities only produces pride and ego.

The natural faith produces confidence in ones abilities but the spiritual faith produces complete trust in God and confidence in your abilities through God and not in yourself. When these two combine, they produce a mountain moving, momentum generating quality [not quantum] of faith. They produce the kind of faith that everyone is look and praying for; the kind of faith God expects us to have. That is the God kind of faith. Faith is a conviction, absolute conviction of the reality of the thing you are hoping for even when there is no physical evidence whatsoever. Where there is lack of confidence and conviction during prayer, affirmation or faith project, there will not be enough faith to bring in the desired result. Be careful, faith is not arrogant, proud, presumptuous, sensual or the like. Faith is concrete conviction in the heart not just by what you say. If you truly don't believe it, you will definitely not have it.

Confidence and assurance are two key ingredients in the exercise of faith. To exercise spiritual faith you must be certain of what you desire and who you believe in. This brings us back to the discussion on the role of the Word of God in using spiritual faith.

One of the things that make it difficult for believers to exercise godly faith is the ignorance of the Word. You must be certain of what the Word of God says and be fully, completely, totally, absolutely, unreservedly and unconditionally convinced and committed to it. Only then will you begin to see miracles on a daily basis. The word of God holds the key to godly prayer answering, miracle working, and mountain moving faith. No man ever worked a miracle by his own power.

Miracles manifest themselves wherever and in whomever there is godly faith. The scripture says "For the word of God is alive and active, sharper than any double-edged sword, it penetrates even to dividing the soul and spirit, joints and marrow; it judges the thoughts and attitudes of the heart" Hebrews 4:12 Jesus said "The Spirit gives life; the flesh counts for nothing. The words I have spoken to you— they are [full of the] Spirit and life.

Faith and Self-Esteem

Self-confidence is a by product of your faith value. Wherever faith is lacking, self confidence and self-esteem will also be lacking; and where there is faith there will be found personal authority, dignity, self-worth, self-expression and vibrant self-esteem and confidence. Faith is not arrogant or boastful because it is a gift. Faith is a settled assurance within. You cannot earn faith but you can cultivate, nurture and nourish it.

I once heard the story of a young woman who because of her poor upbringing and the way she was mistreated and used as a foot mat did not know how beautiful she was until someone paid the highest bride price in the land to marry her. Suddenly she realized that she was worth more than any other girl in the land. Her self-worth grew and her self-esteem rose. You are worth more than you think and you are richer than you know if you have faith confidence. May God give your faith a big boost from now on. Christ has given us His faith so we can become the richest men and women in the land.

One of the advantages of a positive self-image that is based on faith is that it will keep you in times of adversity such as ill-health. Many people who die quickly when they are faced with difficult times and terminal illnesses do so because of loss of faith and self-confidence. You need more faith in hard or bad times than in good times. High or big faith takes time to cultivate and grow. For that reason it is good to seek out the black sheep or goat before dusk because it is harder to find them when darkness falls. Ecclesiastes 12:1 by extrapolation says seek God when you are young and healthy before old age, adversity and ill health come. Your faith, if properly anchored in God, will support and prop you up when you face and go through hard times. You will come out of it fairly quickly and stronger than those who had no faith or were struggling with their faith and low self-image.

The down turns of life sometimes happens very suddenly and do not give enough time for preparation. It is in such situations that people begin to ask 'where is my God? or where was God when all this was happening?' I love the P5 quotation "A prayerful preparation prevents poor performance."

Faith preparation is very important and necessary in the life of every human being especially in the early and young adult periods of life. Scripture Says "Train up a child in the way he should go: and when he is old, he will not depart from it." Proverbs 22:6. It is equally true to train up your faith in the way it should go, so that when you need it, it will not disappoint you. Your 7th Sense is such a rare commodity that it has no substitute. For that reason the evil one seeks always to corrupt it with fear, doubt, unbelief and anxiety. Faith that is not placed on the living God is faith well-misplaced.

Conquering Self-Esteem and Image Problems through Faith

"For God did not give us a spirit of timidity (of cowardice, of craven and cringing and fawning fear), but [He has given us a spirit] of power and of love and of calm and well-balanced mind and discipline and self-control." 2Timothy 1-7. Amplified.

One scripture that give me courage, hope and confidence is the above quote. Rendered in NKJV it says, "For God has not given us the spirit of fear; but of power, and of love, and of a sound mind." This powerful quote always restores my confidence when my self-worth is challenged or I am threatened by fear. The spirit that we received from God is the spirit of boldness. This is what the spirit of God says about us in the scripture. "… but the people that do know their God shall be strong, and do exploits. Daniel 11:32b. Boldness instead of timidity, confidence instead if shyness, courage instead of cowardice and faith instead of fear, these are what God has given to us. Every believer has the potential to rise above his fears and doubts and believe the grace of God to lift him or her up when he is down, depressed, or frustrated with life. Life can be very challenging and our faith is constantly challenged. But when we allow our faith to be robbed, then our confidence and self-esteem take a bigger hit and we succumb to lower self image and self-doubt.

Self-confidence is a product of strong faith in the All-Powerful and Awesome God. Some put this statement in a reverse order, that is, confidence is a product of strong faith in self. But what happens when self is no longer strong as it used to be either through sickness, loss of fortune, old age?, etc. Just as we said before, confidence must be anchored in something or someone greater, higher, bigger, wiser, more durable and longer lasting than self, I mean a true hero. Who is your true hero that cannot ever disappoint?

Who is your true hero? For me Jesus Christ is my true hero. He lived, died and rose again from the dead and conquered death, shame, sickness and disease and has become the true hero for most people. In Him we live and move and have our being. Acts17:28. Therefore, we draw our confidence from His exalted and un-paralleled faith. That is, nothing can defeat us if He who conquered death is standing with us. Listen to what He said in the scripture, "Fear thou not; for I am with thee: be not dismayed; for I am thy God: I will strengthen thee; yea, I will help thee; yea, I will uphold thee with the right hand of my righteousness." Isaiah 41:10. The knowledge of the Almighty is the foundation of a true self-worth.

Confidence Building Scriptures

1. For God has not given us a spirit of fear, but of power and of love and of a sound mind. 2Timothy 1:7

2. God is our refuge and strength, an ever-present help in trouble. Psalm 46:1

3. Rejoice not against me, O mine enemy: when I fall, I shall arise; when I sit in darkness, the LORD shall be a light unto me. Micah 7:8.

4. Trust in the LORD, and do good; dwell in the land, and feed on His faithfulness. Delight yourself also in

the LORD, and He shall give you the desires of your heart. Psalm 37:3-4

5. Commit your way to the LORD, trust also in Him, and He shall bring it to pass. He shall bring forth your righteousness as the light, and your justice as the noonday. Psalm 37:5-6.

6. Rest in the LORD, and wait patiently for Him; do not fret because of him who prospers in his way, because of the man who brings wicked schemes to pass. Cease from anger, and forsake wrath; Do not fret—it only causes harm. For evil doers shall be cut off… Psalm 37:7-9.

7. I have been young, and now am old; yet have I not seen the righteous forsaken, nor his seed begging bread. Psalm 37:25.

8. Mark the perfect man, and behold the upright: for the end of that man is peace. Psalm 37:37.

9. Many are the afflictions of the righteous, but the LORD delivers him out of them all. Psalm 37:19

10. Trust in the LORD with all your heart, and lean not on your own understanding; in all your ways acknowledge Him, and He shall direct your paths. Proverbs 3:5-6.

11. No weapon formed against you shall prosper, and every tongue which rises against you in judgment You shall condemn. This is the inheritance of the

servants of the LORD, and their righteousness is from Me,' says the LORD." Isaiah 54:17.

12. Behold, all they that were incensed against thee shall be ashamed and confounded: they shall be as nothing; and they that strive with thee shall perish. Thou shalt seek them, and shalt not find them, even them that contended with thee: they that war against thee shall be as nothing, and as a thing of naught. For I the LORD thy God will hold thy right hand, saying unto thee, Fear not; I will help thee.

13. The things which are impossible with men are possible with God. Luke 18:27

14. God is not a man, that He should lie. Has He said, and will He not do it? Numbers 23:19

15. But let patience have its perfect work that you may be perfect and complete, lacking nothing. James 1:4

16. If God be for us, who can be against us? Rom 8:31

17. Be strong in the grace that is in Christ Jesus. 2 Timothy 21

18. Set your mind on things above, not on things on the earth. Col 3:2

19. Whatever you do, do it heartily, as to the Lord and not to men,... Colossians 3:23

20. If you can believe, all things are possible to him who believes. Mark 9:23

21. In the world you will have tribulation; but be of good cheer, I have overcome the world. John 16:33

22. Consider that the sufferings of this present time are not worthy to be compared with the glory which shall be revealed in us. Romans 8:18

23. Nothing can separate us from the love of God which is in Christ Jesus our Lord. Rom 8:39

24. And we know that all things work together for good to those who love God, to those who are the called according to His purpose. Romans 8:28

25. Fight the good fight of faith… 1Timothy 6:12

26. I can do all things through Christ who strengthens me. Philipians 4:13

27. You have overcome them, because He who is in you is greater than he that is in the world. 1John 4:4

28. Be confident of this very thing, that He who has begun a good work in you will complete it until the day of Jesus Christ. Philipians 1:6

29. Let us then approach the throne of grace with confidence, so that we may receive mercy and find grace to help us in our time of need Hebrews 4:16.

30. My heart is confident in you, O God, no wonder I can sing your praises Psalm 108:1 NLT

31. Faithful is he that calleth you, who also will do it. [The one who calls you is faithful and He will do it] 2 Thessalonians 5:24.

32. "The Lord is my light and my salvation; whom shall I fear? the Lord is the strength of my life; of whom shall I be afraid?" Psalm 27:1

33. When my father and mother forsake me, then the Lord will take me up. Psalm 27:10

34. Be of good courage, and He shall strengthen your heart, all ye that hope in the Lord. Psalm 31:24

35. In God have I put my trust: I will not be afraid what man can do unto me. Psalm 56:11

36. Though I walk in the midst of trouble, thou wilt revive me: thou shalt stretch forth thine hand against the wrath of mine enemies, and thy right hand shall save me." Psalms 138:7

37. He that dwelleth in the secret place of the most High shall abide under the shadow of the Almighty. I will say of the Lord, He is my refuge and my fortress: my God; in Him will I trust. Psalm 91:1-2

38. He heals the brokenhearted and binds up their wounds [curing their pains and their sorrows. Psalm 147:3

39. "Be careful [anxious] for nothing: but in everything by prayer and supplication with thanksgiving let your requests be made known unto God. And the peace of God, which passeth all understanding, shall keep your hearts and minds through Christ Jesus." Philippians 4:6-7

40. We are troubled on every side, yet not distressed; we are perplexed, but not in despair; persecuted, but not forsaken; cast down, but not destroyed. II Corinthians 4:8-9

41. Let us not be weary in well doing: for in due season we shall reap, if we faint not. Galatians 6:9

42. Now the God of hope fill you with all joy and peace in believing, that ye may abound in hope, through the power of the Holy Ghost. Romans 15:13

43. Therefore do not throw away your confidence, which has a great reward. For you have need of [patience] endurance, so that when you have done the will of God you may receive what is promised. Hebrew 10:35-36.

44. I praise you, for I am fearfully and wonderfully made. Wonderful are your works; my soul knows it very well. Psalm 139:13-14

45. Have I not commanded you? Be strong and courageous. Do not be frightened, and do not be dismayed, for the Lord your God is with you wherever you go." Joshua 1:9

46. No man shall be able to stand before you all the days of your life; as I was with Moses, so I will be with you. I will not leave you nor forsake you. Joshua 1:5.

47. There is no fear in love, but perfect love casts out fear. For fear has to do with punishment, and whoever fears has not been perfected in love. 4:181 John

48. Therefore do not worry about tomorrow, for tomorrow will worry about itself. Each day has enough trouble of its own. Matthew 6:34

49. But he said to me, "My grace is sufficient for you, for my power is made perfect in weakness." Therefore I will boast all the more gladly of my weaknesses, so that the power of Christ may rest upon me. 2 Corinthians 12:9,10

50. ....that your faith might not rest in the wisdom of men but in the power of God. 1 Corinthians 2:5

51. Trust in the Lord with all your heart, and do not lean on your own understanding. In all your ways acknowledge Him and He shall direct your paths. Proverbs 3:5-6

52. Let us then with confidence draw near to the throne of grace, that we may receive mercy and find grace to help in time of need. Hebrews 4:16

53. And we know that all things work together for good to them that love God, to them who are the called according to his purpose. Romans 8:28.

54. The LORD is my light and my salvation; whom shall I fear? The LORD is the strength of my life; of whom shall I be afraid? Psalm 27:1

55. "Blessed is the man who trusts in the Lord, whose trust is the Lord. He is like a tree planted by water, that sends out its roots by the stream, and does not fear when heat comes, for its leaves remain green, and is not anxious in the year of drought, for it does not cease to bear fruit." Jeremiah 17:7-8

56. There is therefore now no condemnation to them which are in Christ Jesus, who walk not after the flesh, but after the Spirit. For the law of the Spirit of life in Christ Jesus hath made me free from the law of sin and death. Romans 8:1-2

57. And this is the confidence that we have toward him, that if we ask anything according to his will he hears us. And if we know that he hears us in whatever we ask, we know that we have the requests that we have asked of him. 1 John 5:14-15.

58. Though the fig tree may not blossom, Nor fruit be on the vines; though the labor of the olive may fail, and the fields yield no food; though the flock may be cut off from the fold, and there be no herd in the stalls—Yet I will rejoice in the LORD, I will joy in the God of my salvation. Habakkuk 3:17-19

59. For the eyes of the LORD run to and fro throughout the whole earth, to show Himself strong on behalf of those whose heart is loyal to Him. 2 Chronicles 16:9.

60. Keep your life free from love of money, and be content with what you have, for he has said, "I will never leave you nor forsake you." Hebrews 13:5

61. But they who wait for the Lord shall renew their strength; they shall mount up with wings like eagles; they shall run and not be weary; they shall walk and not faint. Isaiah 40:31

62. And call upon me in the day of trouble; I will deliver you, and you shall glorify me." Psalm 50:15.

63. Therefore say unto them, Thus saith the Lord GOD; There shall none of my words be prolonged any more, but the word which I have spoken shall be done, saith the Lord GOD. Ezekiel 12:28.

Faith and miracles

"And he did not many mighty works there because of their unbelief." Matthew 13:58.

"And He marveled because of their unbelief." Mark 6:6

"Later He appeared to the eleven as they sat at the table; and He rebuked their unbelief and hardness of heart, because they did not believe those who had seen Him after He had risen." Mark 16:13-15

"But they were broken (pruned) off because of their unbelief (their lack of real faith), and you are established through faith [because you do believe]. So do not become proud and conceited, but rather stand in awe and be reverently afraid." Romans 11:20. Amplified Bible

So we see that they could not enter in because of unbelief.
Hebrews 3:19.

The above scriptures say it all. Even among believers, miracle producing faith is a struggle for many of us unfortunately. Unbelief is a huge issue in the world and even among Christian church goers and believers. We pray, read the Bible, sing songs that build up faith and yet fail to receive mighty miracle producing faith. And I ask, has miracles ceased as some say? Is God still working signs, miracle and wonders today? Is miracle for everyone else or a select few? These and more questions demand urgent personal answers.

If you believe miracles have ceased, then, the case is closed for you and so do not hope for any personal miracles in your life time. If you believe in miracle, there is hope for another one for you. If you believe that miracles are for a select few, you might be fortunate to be among the few. If you believe that God is still in the business of working miracle, signs and wonders, He will visit you in unexpected ways, through unexpected sources and from unexpected persons very shortly. Mark it. As for me I have chosen to believe and will continue to believe that God is actively working miracles in the lives of those who believe and look for it. How about you?

Jesus called the phenomenon "the bread of God's children." He 'replied, "It is not right to take the children's bread and toss it to the dogs." Matthew 15:26. Bread is a staple food for most people. So also is miracle and should be a staple spiritual food for everyone who believes. I believe in miracles because I receive and witness them on a regular basis.

The more we trust and depend on God's absolute power, wisdom and sufficiency without doubt, the more likely we are to see miracles. The longer and more patiently we wait on God's timing the less likely we are to doubt when our miracles have not yet manifested. A miracle is a divine intervention in human affairs. Therefore we have no control over the time of our visitation nor the avenue, channel and instrument that God will use. If you need a miracle, then ask for it, believe that God will keep His Word and wait patiently for it. God wants to heal you, deliver and save you out of that situation and spoil you with his love.

Why do we doubt the word of God? Has He said anything to you personally or through His word and you found Him to be a liar because He did not keep or fulfill His Word? In that case did you do all that He requested you to do faithfully without fail or falling short in some ways? Let us reason for a while to see who is wrong or right. The scripture says "God *is* not a man, that He should lie, Nor a son of man, that He should repent. Has He said, and will

He not do it? Or has He spoken, and will He not make it good? Numbers23:19.

The word of God vouches to the integrity of God that He will do what He says and keep any promise He has made. If you truly and in all honesty have received a word from God, whether spoken or written and kept you own side in all righteousness and honesty and God was unable to do his own part, you are blameless and God has become a liar to you. But if on the other hand as it is written "For whosoever keeps the Law [as a] whole but stumbles and offends in one [single instance] has become guilty of [breaking] all of it, [James 2:10. Amplified] then God cannot be blamed. I find myself always on the losing end whenever I tried to pit my righteousness against God's. For that reason the message of grace resonates with me very greatly.

If however, you have not been completely faithful on your part and have not depended completely and unconditionally on Him to help you or give you a miracle, then you cannot blame God. You can only be justified by faith if you are unable to keep the whole law and you plead for grace. Galatia 3:10-11 "For all who rely on the works of the law are under a curse, as it is written: "Cursed is everyone who does not continue to do everything written in the Book of the Law." Clearly no one who relies on the law is justified before God, because "the righteous shall live by faith."

The scripture says "But the righteousness that is by faith says: "Do not say in your heart, 'Who will ascend into heaven?'" [that is, to bring Christ down] or 'Who will descend into the deep?' [that is, to bring Christ up from the dead). But what does it say? "The word is near you; it is in your mouth and in your heart," that is, the message concerning faith that we proclaim: If you declare with your mouth, "Jesus is Lord," and believe in your heart that God raised him from the dead, you will be saved."

The Amazing Power of Faith

Faith power is the power produced by the use or application of your faith. It could also mean faith potentials and possibilities with you. That power is unlimited and unrestricted unless you begin to doubt. Faith in its purest form can make an iron to float. "As one of them was cutting down a tree, the iron ax head fell into the water. "Oh no, my lord!" he cried out. "It was borrowed!" The man of God asked, "Where did it fall?" When he showed him the place, Elisha cut a stick and threw it there, and made the iron float. "Lift it out," he said. Then the man reached out his hand and took it." In 2 Kings 6:5-7 it reads

In this story an iron axe-head that fell into the water swam and floated to the top of the water. I was brought up in the riverine areas of the Southeastern Nigeria. I did learn to fish and I know firsthand that even a pebble cannot float. If an iron axe-head falls in to the river, it is as good as lost. But by the power of the action of Elisha's faith, the iron came floating to the top of the water. I pray that whatever that represents a lost axe-head in your life will come floating again. The iron came floating because Elisha dared to take a faith action. Had he not applied the power of his faith, that axe head would've been lost probably forever. Granted Elijah was a special kind of prophet. All the same our own challenges might not be like his own. Faith has power.

Faith can divide a sea and make a way where there is no way. In 2 Kings 2:13-14 it reads "Elisha then picked up Elijah's cloak that had fallen from him and went back and stood on the bank of the River Jordan. He took the cloak that had fallen from Elijah and struck the water with it. "Where now is the LORD, the God of Elijah?" he asked. When he struck the water, it divided to the right and to the left, and he crossed over." This is a familiar story with most Christian audience. However, how many people have paused to think of how Elisha was able to divide the Jordan River.

Considering that Elisha was still under the shock of the sudden departure of his master, the unexpected fear, awe and surprise sighting of the heavenly chariots that swept away his master, and the thought and fear of how to cross back to where they came from. He must have stood at the river bank for a while trying to figure out what to do. Faith is the realization of the things we hope for and the evidence of the things that are invisible. As he realized there was no other way to go back and remembering how his master divided the water for them to pass. He took the mantle of his master and spoke out his action as he slammed Elijah's mantle or cloak on the water. The water immediately answered his faith. He would have probably remained there for a day or more had he not decided to act on his faith. Putting our faith to action is what brings the result and not just having faith and sitting on it. Faith has power. Faith has action. When you are faced with an impossible situation that you do not have the natural abilities and resources to solve then turn on your faith-power

Faith can defeat any Goliath standing in your way. In the story of David and Goliath: 1Samuel 17:36-50. David was clearly the under-dog. By any dint of imagination, David stood no chance with a 10-foot giant, but he quickly turned on his faith-power and faith-ability. This made the giant seem like a dwarf to him as he rushed to meet him. David knew by faith that the size of the giant was not anything to be compared with the size and power of his God. Armed with that knowledge rather than Saul's armor, David ran to meet the giant in battle. God is bigger than any giant, mountain or problem you might be facing or will ever face if you will turn on your faith power and trust the God that can never fail or disappoint.

Faith uses what you have to accomplish its purpose. In this story notice that David could not wear even the kings armor because as he said, "he had not proved or tested them. He rather chose to confront the giant with the weapon that he had tested and proved, that is, the power of his faith in his God. David had proved God and known that through faith in the Word of God, all things are possible and nothing shall be impossible. By human statistics, the chances of David killing the giant with one sling shot would be about 1:1,000,000 (one in a million). It wasn't the ordinary stone David shot that killed the giant. It was the faith with which he faced the incredible odd. Faith is the most powerful force in the universe. That is the reason that anyone who lives by faith suffers persecutions because he is or would be a threat to Satan and his kingdom.

Faith can heal any illness. In all my books I have always mentioned this. This is because I am a living witness to the power of healing through faith. Just as faith can make impossible situations possible as per the above examples, it can also heal any sickness including terminal diseases. In the Gospel of Mark: Chapter 1:40-45. "And it happened when He was in a certain city, that behold, a man who was full of leprosy saw Jesus; and he fell on his face and implored Him, saying, "Lord, if You are willing, You can make me clean." Then He put out His hand and touched him, saying, "I am willing; be cleansed." Immediately the leprosy left him. And He charged him to tell no one, "But go and show yourself to the priest, and make an offering for your cleansing, as a testimony to them, just as Moses commanded."

In the above story, the faith with which the sick man approached Jesus was as important as the faith with which Jesus healed him, and even more important because Jesus might not have located him if he did not act. Every sickness is curable because as Jesus said, He is willing always to help those who come to him by faith. Jesus is the same yesterday, today and forever. Hebrews 13:8. He has not changed and will never change. Only those who believe and trust Him completely and absolutely do experience divine healing on a constant basis. One of the ways Jesus heals nowadays is by revelation. When God reveals the true source or cause of your problem you can find a cure for it.

There is such an astonishing power in faith. Sometimes it is difficult to explain and convey this truth in human language. This is because the feelings and emotions that accompany the knowledge and awareness of this truth can hardly be captured in human words. Just like any other spiritual truth, it is mostly understood by those who possess spiritual understanding and are willing to apply it. Faith is as old, if not older than the universe itself, but man has continued to struggle with it ever since. But those who dare to take God at his word have always been rewarded with living faith and miracles.

Faith is so amazing because by applying and receiving the object of your faith you get to share in the divine abilities of God's wisdom and power. You become acquainted with a divine attribute of God and you experience firsthand the God life in you. Everyone has this potential within him or her and everyone can exercise faith anytime, anywhere and anyhow. When faced with situations beyond your natural human abilities, remember that you have the faith-power and God expects you and is waiting for you to use it. You should try also to encourage others to use their faith by you standing on your own faith. This is because as the scripture puts it, "As iron sharpens iron, so one person sharpens another." Proverbs 27:17.

Believing and using your faith helps you to live and walk by faith. Every miracle producing faith must be an active faith. When you believe and don't act on your faith then you are living on passive faith. Don't ever allow anything to shake your faith because it is the only reserve power you have when all else has failed. Faith is the foundation and fountain of a successful, hopeful and happy living. Faith is such an amazing support for life especially in times of difficulty.

Grain-Of-Faith Therapy

And the Lord said, if ye had faith as a grain of mustard seed, ye might say unto this Sycamine tree, Be thou plucked up by the root, and be thou planted in the sea; and it should obey you. Luke 17:6.

Pure faith is real faith. It makes no difference whether it is small or great. In fact Jesus specifically said we do not need too much faith. In the above scripture rendered in the Message Bible, it reads "But the Master said, "You don't need more faith. There is no 'more' or 'less' in faith. If you have a bare kernel of faith, say the size of a poppy seed, you could say to this sycamore tree, 'Go jump in the lake,' and it would do it." Luke 17:6. This is what I call the "Grain-of-Faith" therapy.

The grain-of- faith therapy says that if you have a grain of faith as small as the mustard seed [which is considered to be one of the smallest seeds there is], you can achieve the impossible in real life. You can have what you say or ask for. Jesus said "For verily I say unto you, that whosoever shall say unto this mountain, Be thou removed, and be thou cast into the sea; and shall not doubt in his heart, but shall believe that those things which he saith shall come to pass; he shall have whatsoever he saith. Therefore, I say unto you, what things soever ye desire, when ye pray, believe that ye receive them, and ye shall have them." Mark 11:23-24.

The grain of faith message is all the truth there is about faith. It is faith in the purest form. It is faith that churns out miracles on a daily basis both big and small. Please do not waste your time looking for a big faith; instead concentrate your energy on eliminating those things that can adulterate your faith and make it weak, impotent and ineffective. These things bear repetition: fear, doubt, unbelief, worry, anxiety, impatience, lack of confidence, etc. just for the purposes of emphasis. I call them destroyers and distractions of faith.

In the story alluded to above, Jesus made his disciples understand that they did not need any more faith than they already had but what they needed was the application of their pure faith. Jesus said 'if you had faith...' Did he not know that they already had faith? Of course He knew they already had faith. They were all Israelites, they all believed in the God of their fathers. Jesus had sent them out on preaching missions and they went and preached, healed the sick and cast out demons in people. They couldn't do any of those without faith. What the disciples were asking was bigger faith to do powerful things like Jesus was doing.

Jesus' answer was a simply reassurance that they already possessed enough faith to move trees and mountains. He assured them that though their faith could be small, it could still, command and control nature and elements of nature: trees, rivers, mountains, men, animals, the weather: rain, snow, thunder, tornado, heat, cold, sun, moon, circumstances and situations: sicknesses, diseases, money, death and life, etc. He meant that all these things were within the power of their words if only they could speak and act by (pure) faith.

The scriptures say that life and death are in the power of the tongue. "Death and life are in the power of the tongue: and they that love it shall eat the fruit thereof." Proverbs 18:21. Again the scripture says, "But what does it say? "The word is near you; it is in your mouth and in your heart," that is, the message concerning faith that we proclaim." Romans 10:8. In the same vein, we the believers of today have the power of life and death in our tongue. Pure faith is unhindered faith, undivided faith, unassuming faith and unrestricted faith.

Unadulterated faith is a pure faith that is not mixed with religion, doubt, fear, unbelief, anxiety and worry. Pure faith is what God demands of all believers. If you say you believe, you must have a high level of unadulterated faith. Without that you will be struggling with basic understanding and application of faith. Unadulterated faith produces pure faith which is the spiritual faith and God's kind of faith. It is faith without blemish. It is the faith that brings instant answers to prayers that everyone is yearning for. "Now the purpose of the commandment is love from a pure heart, from a good conscience, and from sincere (pure, genuine) faith." 1Timothy 1:5.

Unadulterated faith is also faith that is placed squarely on Jehovah the God of heaven and earth. It is the faith that does not consider and would not meddle with faith in any other gods. It is faith that is 100% devoted and concentrated on Jehovah through Jesus Christ. There is no mixing of any other thing to it. It is clean and pure.

God is jealous of His name, reputation, integrity and glory. He says, "I am the LORD: that is my name: and my glory will I not give to another, neither my praise to graven (carved) images. Isaiah 42:8. In Isaiah 48:11, He repeated the same thing; "For mine own sake, even for mine own sake, will I do it: for how should my name be polluted (defamed)? And I will not give my glory unto another." God will honor faith that honors Him.

Adulterated faith is the faith that is weak and double minded. It is the faith that is laden with fear, doubt, unbelief and presumption and not real knowledge of God. Far too many believers possess faith adulterated by sin and that explains why most believers find it difficult to do or receive exceptional miracles and that includes yours humbly. The purpose of this book is to challenge our faith to rise up and reach out for the highest and purest faith that we already possess and to begin to use and apply them for our own good and the benefit of others.

FAITH AND POSSIBLITY THINKING

Here are some simple faith builders:

1. All things are possible and nothing shall be impossible to him that believes.
2. Every problem has an answer and no situation is without a solution.
3. The solution you seek lies buried within you through faith.
4. The solution depends on how you perceive and react to the problem.
5. The solution depends on your mental attitude, emotional adjustment and faith-ability.
6. Possibility thinking and positive mindset are required for positive faith results.
7. Faith thinkers are possibility thinkers. Doubt thinkers are failure thinkers.
8. You do not have a problem to solve; you only have a decision and a faith-choice to make. The choices

and decisions you make in life, affect the outcomes of the problems you face.

9. We are created to create solutions. You have the abilities of God to create and invent solutions.

10. No condition is permanent. Every situation is a passing phase and every phase will come to an end. As it came one day so will it go away another day.

11. Life is lived in phases of positives and negatives but your faith can turn the negatives into positives.

12. Always maintain a right mental attitude that better days are about to begin and good times are around the corner.

13. If God is on your side, whatever is yours will surely come to you.

14. Believe it or not you will win the battle of life. You will overcome your present situation. Hold on to God and trust Him with a pure faith.

15. God will not allow you to be put to shame because you believe in his mercy.

16. Believe in yourself, work hard intelligently and success will come knocking.

17. A faith-full man will not be defeated even if he falls many times.

18. You have the power and the authority of your faith to challenge your giants.

19. If God is for you who can defeat you?

20. Nobody has a money problem; it is always an idea and faith problem.
21. You can make the best out of a little and something out of nothing through faith.
22. The downfall of a man is not the end of his life; you can still become who you want to be if you believe you can.
23. Whatever your mind can conceive and believe, you can achieve.
24. Problem times are tough times. Tough times never last but tough people with tough faith do.
25. Faith is the master key that unlocks all spiritual doors.
26. Faith is not the easy way out but the sure way through.
27. Faith is a living seed if it is properly sown in God. The Word of God is a fertile soil to grow your faith.
28. Faith is a developed ability and a conditioned state of mind to trust and not doubt.
29. Faith is elastic; you can stretch to its farthest limits
30. Without faith you cannot give to God and cannot receive from Him.
31. Faith is the developed ability to influence nature and obtain what is rightfully yours.
32. Faith is being willing to be used by God to accomplish his purposes.
33. Faith continues where other senses stop or fail.

34. Faith relies on four immutable things: the Word of God, the integrity of God, the power and ability of God and the promises of God.

35. Four things that make faith to work: hearing the word of faith, speaking the word of faith, believing the Word you confess and acting on the Word of faith.

36. Your faith will expose you to and manifest your undiscovered gifts, talents, potentials and hidden powers.

37. Your future greatness depends on your ability to apply and use your faith-power.

38. Faith will not break you but will make you better and more confident.

39. Faith is power without borders. Faith can reach where no other sense can go.

40. Purpose directed and purpose driven faith accomplished miraculous things.

41. The opposite side of failure is success as indecision is the seed of failure.

42. Change your failure/poverty mentality with firm decisions to take action on your faith projects.

44. Faith is the compass of the soul. As the airplane cannot go far without a compass so humans cannot see God without faith.

Miscellaneous

Your life should not be defined by your circumstances; your life should be defined by your Faith-ability. Faith is a complete acceptance of truth which may or may not be demonstrated or proved by the process of logical thinking.

Natural faith is limited because it does not understand spiritual things. Spiritual faith is, therefore, superior, unlimited and higher and should be desired. "But the natural man does not receive [understand] the things of the Spirit of God, for they are foolishness to him; nor can he know them, because they are spiritually discerned." 1Corinthians2:14.

When mixed with any emotions, faith produces momentum and increases drive and powerful vibrations of thought. The increased vibrations or spiritual energy equals or supersedes the desire for which it was activated. When that happens, the action taken toward the realization reverberates in the spiritual realms and creates and/or compels an answer from the Infinite.

Prayer is a direct presentation and repetition of desires that have been emotionalized with definite purpose through the channel of faith to the Divine Intelligence. Prayers that are easily answered are said with actionable words.

Prayer is the expression of your thoughts and needs into words of action and channeling them to God through faith. Faith is intentional belief and action. Pray until you believe and continue until something happens.

Prayers do not influence God but they affect Him, therefore choose or use words that will make impact on Him. God has a mind. When prayers affect God, He acts.

There is no such thing as luck. There is only grace and fortune. You either have grace for something and, therefore, fortunate or you don't which is rather unfortunate but you can ask for what you don't have.

Have faith in God and approach Him by faith. Action words and verbs appeal to God in prayer.

If you perceive that you do not have grace for a given task, then ask for it or quit and don't rely on luck because luck is for those who have no faith.

Faith is an active or action word. To have faith you must be actively committed to the task on hand. Faith is the beginning of all success and achievement. Lack of faith is the beginning of all failures.

Faith is the only avenue through which the supernatural powers and resources of the Divine can be accessed and utilized at will.

Every human has the natural propensity, ability and capacity to believe and have faith unless he or she chooses to say I can't or I don't. Directed and pin-pointed faith will make every problem or situation crackle.

CHAPTER 17

THE FAITH CHAPTER

Hebrews 11

Now faith is the substance of things hoped for, the evidence of things not seen. For by it the elders obtained a good testimony.

By faith we understand that the worlds were framed by the word of God, so that the things which are seen were not made of things which are visible.

Faith History

By faith Abel offered to God a more excellent sacrifice than Cain, through which he obtained witness that he was righteous, God testifying of his gifts; and through it he being dead still speaks.

By faith Enoch was taken away so that he did not see death, "and was not found, because God had taken him"; for before he was taken he had this testimony, that he pleased God. But without faith *it is* impossible to please Him, for he who comes to God must believe that He is, and that He is a rewarder of those who diligently seek Him.

By faith Noah, being divinely warned of things not yet seen, moved with godly fear, prepared an ark for the saving of his household, by which he condemned the world and became heir of the righteousness which is according to faith.

Faithful Abraham

By faith Abraham obeyed when he was called to go out to the place which he would receive as an inheritance. And he went out, not knowing where he was going. By faith he dwelt in the land of promise as *in* a foreign country, dwelling in tents with Isaac and Jacob, the heirs with him of the same promise; for he waited for the city which has foundations, whose builder and maker *is* God.

By faith Sarah herself also received strength to conceive seed, and she bore a child when she was past the age, because she judged Him faithful who had promised. Therefore from one man and him as good as dead, were born *as many* as the stars of the sky in multitude—innumerable as the sand which is by the seashore.

Hope in Faith

These all died in faith, not having received the promises, but having seen them afar off were assured of them, embraced *them* and confessed that they were strangers and pilgrims on the earth. For those who say such things declare plainly that they seek a homeland. And truly if they had called to mind that *country* from which they had come out, they would have had opportunity to return. But now they desire a better, that is, a heavenly country. Therefore God is not ashamed to be called their God, for He has prepared a city for them.

The Ancient Fathers

By faith Abraham, when he was tested, offered up Isaac, and he who had received the promises offered up his only begotten son, of whom it was said, "In Isaac your seed shall be called, concluding that God was able to raise him up, even from the dead, from which he also received him in a figurative sense."

By faith Isaac blessed Jacob and Esau concerning things to come.

By faith Jacob, when he was dying, blessed each of the sons of Joseph, and worshiped, leaning on the top of his staff.

By faith Joseph, when he was dying, made mention of the departure of the children of Israel and gave instructions concerning his bones.

The Faith of Moses

By faith Moses, when he was born, was hidden three months by his parents, because they saw *he was* a beautiful child; and they were not afraid of the king's command.

By faith Moses, when he became of age, refused to be called the son of Pharaoh's daughter, choosing rather to suffer affliction with the people of God than to enjoy the passing pleasures of sin, esteeming the reproach of Christ greater riches than the treasures in Egypt; for he looked to the reward.

By faith he forsook Egypt, not fearing the wrath of the king; for he endured as seeing Him who is invisible. By faith he kept the Passover and the sprinkling of blood, lest he who destroyed the firstborn should touch them.

By faith they passed through the Red Sea as by dry land, whereas the Egyptians, attempting to do so, were drowned.

Exploits of Faith

By faith the walls of Jericho fell down after they were encircled for seven days. By faith the harlot Rahab did not perish with those who did not believe, when she had received the spies with peace.

And what more shall I say? For the time would fail me to tell of Gideon and Barak and Samson and Jephthah, also of David and Samuel and the prophets: who through faith subdued kingdoms, worked righteousness, obtained promises, stopped the mouths of lions, quenched the violence of fire, escaped the edge of the sword, out of weakness were made strong, became valiant in battle, turned to flight the armies of the aliens. Women received their dead raised to life again.

Others were tortured, not accepting deliverance, that they might obtain a better resurrection. Still others had trial of mockings and scourgings, yes, and of chains and imprisonment. They were stoned, they were sawn in two, were tempted, were slain with the sword. They wandered about in sheepskins and goatskins, being destitute, afflicted, tormented— of whom the world was not worthy. They wandered in deserts and mountains, in dens and caves of the earth.

And all these, having obtained a good testimony through faith, did not receive the promise, God having provided something better for us, that they should not be made perfect apart from us.

CHAPTER 18

FAITH DECLARATIONS

Faith that brings result

The faith that brings results or receives answers must be faith that declares strong affirmations and declarations of your desired objective or projective. Faith works with words and actions that strengthen it. Positive declarations do just that.

Affirmations of faith are powerful assertions and declarations voiced with faith and authority. They have the potentials to change or effect a change in your situation. There are different types of affirmations that reinforce faith. Below are some declarations:

1. My faith is my power; my power is God's power and is irresistible.
2. My word is my power; my power is God's power and is formidable and irresistible. [Pray]

3. My faith is my power; therefore I will speak boldly, fearlessly and courageously. [Pray]

4. My faith is my power; therefore, I can change my unhappy situation by speaking to it. [Pray]

5. My word is the word of faith filled with blessings; I will bless and not curse. [Pray]

6. My faith is the faith of God and it's automatic. [Pray]

7. My hands are filled with blessings and anyone I touch by faith shall be blessed. [Pray]

8. My word is my power and it's filled with miraculous authority. [Pray]

9. My faith is my power; it shall justify and not condemn me. [Pray]

10. I am a spirit being; I can create the world I choose to live in. [Pray]

11. I am a spirit being, therefore my mind is under subjection and my body is under control by faith. [Pray]

12. I can do all things through faith in God who strengthens me. [Pray]

13. All things are possible to Him that believes. I believe, therefore, I live in my own world of possibilities. [Pray]

14. I possess a miraculous faith bank, it shall never run dry; as I give and as I spend I receive more. [Pray]

15. I possess an inexhaustible faith wallet/purse which can never run dry; it is packed and filled with

currencies in $1000 dollar equivalent denominations. [Pray]

16. I have a divine faith-account with the bank of heaven. It can never be depleted. As I draw it is instantly replenished so that I always have a surplus. [Pray]

17. By faith I have now received the resurrection dominion over sicknesses and diseases and all things are subject to me. [Pray]

18. I have a divine mind by faith and I receive daily illuminations and revelations. [Pray]

19. By faith I will tap into divine resources and supply today and all my needs shall be met with divine favor and providence.

20. My faith is strong; therefore, I recognize no limitations stopping me from reaching my divine destiny because I am fearfully and wonderfully made.

21. I have the advantage of the 7th Sense and I see all obstacles on my way and overcome them by my faith.

22. By faith I rise above all negative emotions: unbelief, envy, hatred, fear, doubt, worry, anger, un-forgiveness, resentment and other negative emotions that weigh down my spirit and reduce my ability to operate on the level of the 7th Sense. I silence them by the actions of my faith.

23. I have an endless and unlimited divine source of supply and all my needs are met expressly by faith.

24. Though I walk through the valley of the shadow of death I will fear no evil for the Lord is with me.

25. I am a child of the Most High, no power on earth can destroy me, and no power on earth can subdue me.

26. I stand on my divine platform of faith which is now cleared for miraculous action and intervention in every area of my life.

27. I banish every dark cloud that limits my 100% vision in the spirit realm; I can now see clearly though the eyes of my faith.

28. I see no challenges and there are no obstacles in the divine mind; whatever good opportunities I have lost shall be recovered by faith in miraculous ways.

29. There is set before me the miraculous open door of faith which no man can shut because it is sustained by The Blood.

30. The faithful are as bold as the lion; therefore, I am more than a conqueror through faith in God.

31. By divine mandate, my seemingly impossible and difficult situations are now made easy in unexplainable ways by faith.

32. My faith now sees and lives in the positive and sunny side of life and all my negative past is banished forever.

33. By faith I reject and refuse to live in the negative side of life anymore.

34. Those that know their God shall be strong and do exploit; therefore I am bold, strong and irresistible.

35. I now have the power of faith; I therefore, command every door to open before me. As one door closes another door opens instantly before me.

36. The joy of the Lord is my strength; therefore I am happy, loving, cheerful and irresistible.

37. I have the mandate of God to exercise dominion over all things; therefore, by faith I control all circumstances and situations around me.

38. By my faith I banish every evil storms of life blowing across my pathway.

39. I possess within me many undiscovered gifts, talents, abilities and graces which are now revealed to me by faith in unexplainable ways.

40. I receive my open doors of success and destiny and no man can shut them for they are sealed with The Blood.

41. There is no struggle or rivalry in the realms of the spirit and all that is mine shall come to me by faith and in their good time.

42. I have the miraculous power of faith within me; whatever I decree by faith shall come to pass.

43. I now live in the endless world of new opportunities and divine graces, by faith I live triumphantly over my enemies.

44. I am a carrier of the divine presence of God's healing power; therefore, by faith, I am healed.

45. By faith I turn every difficulty/obstacle is a stepping ladder, every hindrance a springboard, every limitation a blessings-pack and every disappointment a launching-pad to my destiny.

46. By faith Christ's divine purposes are established in my life; they are permanent, irreversible and no power can change them.

47. Heaven is turned loose on my behalf and all good things that I desire now begin to flow to me from all directions.

48. There are now new arenas of divine actions and blessings blossoming before me, I now enter into my season of rest.

49. The royal broadways of faith, success and peace are now open before me; I can see my destiny being fulfilled in spectacular and miraculous ways.

50. Faith is the assurance and the evidence of things hoped for, therefore, my faith-desires shall come to pass in record time.

51. My faith shall supply all my needs according to divine resource in God's glory.

52. Hear the word of the faith. The lord our God is one Lord.

53. I live by my active faith and all that belong to me shall gravitate to me under divine guidance.

54. My faith is built and anchored on a solid rock; therefore I cannot fall though all around me are sinking.

55. Every person in my life is there for a purpose both the good and the bad; they help to bring out the best in me and fulfill God's purpose in my life.

56. My faith is increasing, my hope is sure and my blessings are on their way to establish me with favor.

57. My faith is my power; my power is God's power and is without borders. It reaches to the highest mountains, it flows to the lowest valleys and therefore, I cannot be limited.

58. I live by grace, practice love, teach the truth and walk by faith, therefore I am unstoppable.

59. Those who pursue new adventures all through life stay young, think better, laugh louder and live longer. That is me.

60. Eye has not seen, ear has not heard and it has never been revealed to anyone what I shall become through faith in Christ Jesus.

61. The devil wanted me to be afraid and I asked him "between me and you who should be afraid of the other and he said 'I' (devil). Then I asked why and

he said "Because you carry the fire of the Holy One by faith."

62. My life is not defined by my present circumstances and situations but by my faith-abilities.

63. Where fear abounds, faith abounds the more, therefore, I will overcome my fears with my faith.

64. The plan of God for my life cannot be changed, aborted or destroyed; I receive faith with grace to fulfill my destiny.

THE END

ABOUT THE BOOK

- This book is powerful and thought-provoking. There is a steady rhythm and cadence to the writing and the overall pace of the book is good. Overall length of the book is appropriate.
- The author is a seasoned writer, whose tone is impassioned, authoritative and inspirational.
- The conclusion is strong and effectively wraps up loose ends while showcasing the main message.
- The author strives to provide clarity for the reader, and does so with detailed explanations, definitions, and literary tools like metaphors, similes and other relevant examples.
- Chapter titles are short, to the point and accurate reflections of their inner contents.
- The author provides scriptures and Bible references to substantiate and illustrate the biblical basis for each point to the audience.
- It is our belief that you have enjoyed and will enjoy reading this book.

Manuscript Review

ABOUT THE AUTHOR

Humphrey Akparah is a gifted writer, Bible teacher, spiritual counselor, motivational speaker and deliverance minister. As a church planter, he founded two churches in Africa and was instrumental in other church planting and equipping. He is also a personal coach for individuals who want to write and publish their own books and he facilitates creative writing workshops for groups, schools and organizations.

This author has written three other powerful inspirational books collectively called: The Amazing Book Series and more are yet to be published. The Books are:

1. The Amazing Power of Grace
2. The Amazing power of Faith
3. Authority of the Excellent Name of Jesus

He is available for consultations.

To contact the author:

Email: amazzingbooks@yahoo.com;
           humpphreyakparah@yahoo.com
           humphreyakparah444@gmail.com
Phone: 1-403-918-2011
http://christianreading.com//hakparah